Blind for a Purpose

Turning Life-challenges Into Purpose In Life

Written By

Blake Andrew Lindsay

IBW Publishing
www.ibwpublishing.com

Blind for a Purpose: Turning Life-challenges into Purpose in Life

Blake A. Lindsay

ISBN: 978-0-9847596-0-6
Library of Congress Control Number: to come

1. Self-Help: Motivational & Inspirational
2. Self-Help: Personal Growth – Success
3. Self-Help: Spiritual

Copyright © 2011

Scripture taken from the HOLY BIBLE, NEW INTERNATIONAL VERSION®. Copyright © 1973, 1978, 1984 by International Bible Society. Used by permission of Zondervan Publishing House. All rights reserved.

All rights reserved. No part of this book may be reproduced without written permission from the publisher, except by a reviewer who may quote brief passages in a review; nor may any part of this book be reproduced, stored in a retrieval system or transmitted in any form without written permission from the publisher.

This book is manufactured in the United States of America.

Testimonials

"Blake Lindsay has a passion for what he does only surpassed by his talent! The professionalism and polish of the Ziglar podcast as well as the other audio projects we have done with Blake are a testimony to his hard work and expertise. Blake is truly a difference maker in this arena!" - Tom Ziglar

"Blind for a Purpose" will inspire, motivate and encourage you. No matter where you are in your life, you'll identify with Blake's life. The lessons Blake shares will touch your heart and your head. You'll be glad you invested your time." - Bryan Flanagan, President Flanagan Training Group (Blake's Buddy)

"I found Blake Lindsay's book to be delightful reading. It "sounds" just like him. He makes it very easy for the reader to paint mind pictures as he relates stories from his life and experiences. It's just fun, encouraging and entertaining reading." - Laurie Magers, Executive Assistant to Zig Ziglar

"Blake is one of the happiest people I know--and I know him well. I've interviewed him on the radio, spent the weekend with him, prayed with him, and talked to him for hundreds of hours. He truly is one of the happiest I know. I hope you get a hold of what he has to share in this book" – James A. Smith, Founder, IWasBornToWin.com

"I first met Blake working for KODZ, an Oldies radio station in Dallas, Texas. What a blast we had! This is a time which I will always treasure. I am honored to call Blake Lindsay my friend.
Thank you for taking the time to help me relive some wonderful memories!" - Mark Whitcomb (aka Marconi the Madman), Case Manager - The Salvation Army, Dallas/Ft. Worth

Dedication

This book is dedicated to my loving parents,
Dr. Larry and Gail Lindsay, as well as to my four siblings,
Brad, Molly, Bryce and Brock. Thank you for your individual contributions in helping me to live a normal life.
I now "see" things even more clearly through the writing of this book.

"... With God all things are possible." Matthew 19:26

Table of Contents

Testimonials 3
Foreword 6
Introduction 8
Chapter 1 In The Beginning 9
Chapter 2 Sight-Full Siblings 13
Chapter 3 Glorious School Days 17
Chapter 4 Navigating Through Darkness 27
Chapter 5 Blind Boy Scouts 31
Chapter 6 Blake and His Cycles 33
Chapter 7 Blake Goes to Camp 39
Chapter 8 Summer School Memories 41
Chapter 9 Music Man 45
Chapter 10 Blake the Swimmer 49
Chapter 11 God's Protection 55
Chapter 12 My CB Radio 61
Chapter 13 Blake's Broadcast Career 63
Chapter 14 Baseball Blake for the Afternoon 77
Chapter 15 The Real World of Business 81
Chapter 16 Bringing Your "A" Game to Life's Challenges 83
Chapter 17 New York City 85
Chapter 18 Jennifer 87
Chapter 19 Transformation 91
Chapter 20 Leap of Faith 95
Chapter 21 The Power of Prayer 99
Chapter 22 Seeing Beyond the Blindness 103
Chapter 23 Living as a Christian 109
Final Thoughts 113
Further Information 115

Foreword

Blind for a Purpose will open your eyes and your heart in a truly remarkable and encouraging way. Blake Lindsay's writing is forthright, heartfelt and "right on" in every way. As you read what Blake has to say about being blind, I believe you will come to clearly understand that his "vision" is truly remarkable. Chances are good you have your sight, particularly if you are reading the book! But I am excited to be able to say that I honestly believe your vision will be dramatically broadened; your life will be changed and enriched in a dramatic way as you read Blake's story.

Having known Blake and his family for many years, I can tell you they are real—they are solid. This is a production of bedrock America at its best. You will be inspired, encouraged and undoubtedly find a new lease on your own life in many ways. I believe you will find *Blind for a Purpose* to be well worth the read—and even subsequent re-reads! It's good—really good!

Zig Ziglar,
Author and Motivational Teacher,
Dallas, Texas

For My Readers:

May my stories in this book make you laugh, smile and appreciate the true beauty of life and all that it has to offer.
May they also bring you hope, joy, and a sense of purpose.
It is my hope that through this book you will appreciate having your eyes wide open even more today than you did yesterday.

This is my story…

Introduction

Blind people are normal. Each of us encounters challenges and hurdles in life to leap over and learn from. As I share my experiences with you, I hope that you can gain a sense of my gratefulness for life and my appreciation for God allowing the right doors to open for me. I believe you will come to understand my expanded optimism for others who endure raising a child with extra challenges and for those of you who have additional obstacles to overcome. It is fulfilling to know that through my positive attitude and best efforts in the workplace, God has enabled many others to see the true light through my loss of sight.

Most of my inspiration comes from my parents, who chose to raise me in a Christian environment and to view my blindness as a blessing, not a hindrance. They enabled me to face challenges and motivate others to be the best they can.

Mom and Dad also introduced me to Zig Ziglar, a nationally recognized motivational Christian man who has not only become my encouraging friend and mentor, but has also touched hundreds of thousands of lives throughout the world with his optimistic and life-changing approach.

As you read this book, my journey continues. I am eager to find out what God has in store for the rest of my life. Even as a blind man I can clearly see that great things will happen. I have learned the benefits of inner joy and optimism, knowing that the best is truly yet to come.

Chapter **1** In The Beginning

I am Blake Andrew Lindsay and I am totally blind. I am the only one of five children in my family to be sightless and was born to sighted parents. There is no history of blindness in my family. I was born on August 21, 1964, and nine months later it was discovered that I had a cancerous and potentially life-threatening disease called retinoblastoma. Up until then I had complete sight.

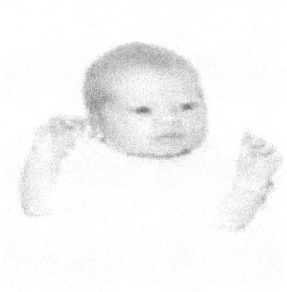

This is before I lost my sight at a very young age. I have no memory of those days.

My parents were in their mid twenties when my condition was diagnosed. At age seventeen, I remember as if it were today, Mom and Dad sat me down and carefully explained all of the details regarding their rare experience. My mother was the first to notice my lack of alertness during feeding times and a cloudy appearance in my eyes. Her motherly instincts told her that something was definitely wrong. Not wasting any time, my parents took me to our family doctor, an eye doctor, and then to a nationally renowned specialist. It was a bit of a whirlwind for my Mom and Dad.

Our family doctor diagnosed possible strabismus. The eye doctor was more concerned and considered that it might be a detached retina but wanted me to see a specialist. Within a few days I was examined by a team of doctors at the Indiana University Medical Center in Indianapolis where the diagnosis of retinoblastoma was made. This of course was quite a shock for my parents, grandparents, relatives, and friends. Not only was I going to be sightless, but also my family was in a rush to keep cancer from harmfully spreading to my brain through my optic nerves and taking my life.

Mom and Dad were tactfully informed that the prescription to save my life was to remove my eyes at the optic nerve as soon as possible. After hearing those terrifying but crucial facts, my parents quickly inquired about the possibility of transplanting one of their eyes with the hope that their contributions would save my sight.

Despite their willingness and generosity, they learned that their loving offer was not going to benefit me in any way. It is my understanding this type of surgery is not helpful even today. The tremendous impact which I have received over the years from knowing my young parents would do anything in their capacity to salvage my sight has benefited me greatly in a completely different and wonderful way.

By age seventeen, and even more throughout my adult life, I realized how much my parents were willing to share and sacrifice in doing their best to make certain I could have the same benefits as most people. This has also taught me the significance of generosity. I also learned that when our lives make a drastic and unexpected turn, one which occasionally leads us right into a rough region, I will try to think of everything I can feasibly do. Just like the genuine contribution and sacrifice my parents were prepared to make. This, without a doubt, has helped me to focus on any positive aspect I can find in whatever negative circumstances I am facing.

That talk with my parents was, and still is, an emotional moment for me. I imagine what it would be like to trade places with them and actually have been in their traumatic situation. Today as an adult, when I reflect on their experience, I am deeply appreciative for having heard all of the facts and my parents' feelings regarding our unique and challenging family event.

One benefit of my situation is the big smile I experience each time I consider, as a grown man, that here I was not even a full year old and my parents had already established four classic examples for me. First, they demonstrated how to respond with poise and confidence to shocking news rather than reacting in complete panic when faced with devastating information. Mom and Dad had to function in great faith, believing that God was in complete control. Second is that my parents have always communicated that God would use me and my testimony to benefit others facing life-challenges or family catastrophe.

Third, Mom and Dad showed me that in most devastating situations; the worst part will pass quickly. Finally, my parents proved to me the importance of staying proactive and always believing that the best is yet to come. The wonderful ways which their extraordinary story has encouraged me and taught me through most of my adult life has evolved into my sense of gratitude for how God has saved me and prepared me to be able to share my story of hope and love with prayerfully millions of people.

With the specialists' final diagnosis, my optical nerves were quickly removed - leaving me 100% sightless. Since I have no recollection of seeing and have lived most of my entire life without the capability to see, I have rarely felt sorry for myself. I am thankful that my eyesight was all that was taken and my life was spared. It feels great to be alive!

Chapter 2 Sight-Full Siblings

Fifteen months prior to my birth, my parents welcomed to the world a healthy, eight pound, two ounce, baby boy named Bradley Kent. He was eager to become a big brother and even though I was blind, it did not hinder him one bit from showing me the ropes. When I was a year old he took me by the hand and taught me how to walk.

The family legacy continued. My vigorous sister, Molly Paige, was born 16 days before my fifth birthday. I was excited to join the ranks with Brad on becoming a big brother. I remember how special it was to have a sister in our family of five. Molly had a fascination with the television set and before she turned one, she had mastered the skill of being able to turn it on with ease; highly impressing me. Ironically, as an adult Molly rarely watches television.

Molly impressed me in other ways as well. The summer she turned five and I turned ten, my young sister took me on walks around our small town. We felt independent and enjoyed breathing in the fresh air.

Molly was the best little sister that anyone could ever ask for and I was fortunate that she was mine. We did, however, have our daredevil sides; she helped me roller skate. Molly would get on her tricycle and I would put on my infamous wheeled-shoes. I held on tightly as Molly *zoomed* her 85-pound brother happily around the block. She was a speedster and I was having a blast. Dad clocked Molly before her sixth birthday buzzing along at 14 miles per hour. We were all surprised at how fast her young legs could pedal. Go, Molly, go!

While I was growing up and attending a school for blind and low vision students, Molly became my right-hand. Each winter she accompanied me to several houses as I sold fruitcakes for the PTA. Our adventures in sales did not end there. Our winning team efforts

The Lindsay kids in 1978. That's 13-year-old me holding Brock with eight-year-old Molly by my side. Brad, who was 14 at the time, is holding Bryce, not yet four.

13

also brought us opportunities to sell candy bars, popcorn, and numerous items to family, friends, and neighbors. I enjoy recalling the time spent together and the many successes we shared.

The same summer that Molly pulled me around on my roller skates I became a big brother *again*. I will never forget what I was doing when mom announced that she and Dad needed to leave for the hospital, as it was time for the newest Lindsay family member to arrive. Jim Nabors might be delighted to know that I was listening to a *Gomer Pyle* rerun, one of my favorite old TV shows.

Everyone predicted that the newest addition to the Lindsay household would be a boy, and their predictions were correct. Bryce Inwood was born at 6:53 p.m. on August 8, 1974, three days after Molly's birthday. Thirteen days before mine and on the day President Richard Nixon resigned. The largest Lindsay baby weighed eight pounds, 12 ounces, and was 23 inches long.

Four days after Bryce's birth, I finally got to meet my brand new little brother, who I refer to now in my adult life as "Big-B."

Following my thirteenth birthday, my parents called all four of us kids together for a family huddle. They shared with us some unanticipated, yet exciting news. In January, just five months later, another addition would be joining the Lindsay family. No one anticipated the excitement surrounding the birth of the fifth Lindsay.

Mom and Dad became increasingly concerned as a fierce storm was making its presence very near to the predicted moment the fifth Lindsay child was to make his or her grand appearance. A few feet of snow is typical in Central Indiana during the winter months, but on January 25, 1978, the wind began to blow and the snow really started to fall. With forecasters predicting more unusually severe weather on the way, it was safer for me to stay the night at the blind school so that my parents did not have to make the thirteen-mile trek in severe weather. Snow continued to fall and the wind continued to blow. With a whopping 14 inches now on the ground, the wind chill factor made it feel like forty below zero.

With Mom nearly in labor and quick to get the situation under control, my parents called our local fire department, as it was equipped with four-wheel drive vehicles that could safely transport people in the worst of conditions—particularly those needing to get to a hospital. Upon the arrival of two fire fighters, Jim Smith and Gary Southerland, my parents were assured they were trained to deliver babies in emergencies.

After carefully assessing the situation, everyone decided to load up Mom and Dad and drive them to the nearest hospital in Noblesville, eight miles from our home. Late that wintry Wednesday night when most people were tucked in their beds, with extra covers pulled up to their heads, in came the emergency team. With my parents in tow the team made their way in a balloon tired, 4-wheel vehicle that actually rode over, rather than through, the deep snow. Although the emergency crew was not able to discern the exactness of the roadsides or turns, the journey to the hospital was successfully completed to the great relief of my parents and members of our family.

About forty hours later, Brock Wyatt Lindsay, eight pounds and two ounces, was born at 5:00 PM just in time for dinner in the midst of the notorious blizzard of '78. This particular birth was extremely special to my mother, as her vision of having a large family was made even more a reality. I'm glad that my parents' traumatic and memorable experience of me becoming blind from cancerous tumors did not detour their desire to have more children and grow our family. Mom and Dad now had four sons and one daughter.

Coincidentally, my dad was experiencing another rare reality. As a result of the blizzard, the hospital was short of staff. My father, having earned his Doctorate in Educational Administration (Ed.D.) approximately a year prior to Brock's birth, was officially referred to as "Dr. Lindsay" by educators, businessmen, and friends. The hospital asked my dad if he would be willing to lend a helping hand to assist with medical emergencies. He reminded them he did not have a medical doctorate degree. The hospital staff, though desiring a medical doctor, did not let my dad off the hook. Instead, my dad put on some scrubs as any doctor would and began his rotation with a critical procedure … washing dishes in the hospital cafeteria.

Chapter 3 Glorious School Days

At age four, I was off to York Preschool, an enjoyable experience. Young children are often oblivious to other children who are different from them. My sighted classmates were no exception. We interacted well and I made many friends.

I do not recall many of the children questioning me about being blind. Perhaps that was partly due to the way my teacher, Mrs. Regan, interacted with me. Even though Mrs. Regan did not regularly have students with physical disabilities, she had plenty of experience dealing with blindness. She had a stepson, Dennis, who was also totally blind. Dennis was six years older than me so my teacher was quite comfortable dealing with my condition. Because of this commonality she and I shared, we formed a special bond. I even kept in touch with her until I became a teenager.

After my fifth birthday, I was enrolled into the Indiana School for the Blind. Prior to this, the only blind person I had been exposed to was me, myself, and I. I was excited to meet other kids who could completely relate with me on what it was like to be visually impaired. With this overwhelming feeling of excitement also came a sense of nervousness and uncertainty. Had it really mattered that I had not been exposed to other sightless people? Was a change in schools really going to help five-year-old Blake Andrew Lindsay?

"Powerful, life changing, and meaningful" are the words I use to describe the years from kindergarten through tenth grade while attending the Indiana School for the Blind. I received an excellent education and gained fruitful new friendships. This school setting brought together visually impaired students from all over the state of Indiana who were totally blind like me, and also those with low vision. Some of the students lived quite a distance from the school and opted to stay in the dormitories. For the better part of the first five years I attended the Blind school. I was a daily commuter, which I preferred, as I did not want to miss any of Mom's extraordinarily good cooking at dinnertime. I did eat the school lunch, but I will not exaggerate about the superiority of our cafeteria food. Thinking back, I usually had perfect attendance so the meals prepared by the lunch ladies couldn't have been all that bad.

I remember the first day of first grade as if it were yesterday. I still chuckle to myself when I recall meeting Kevin Sparks for the first time. It all came about when I happened to feel his hair that day. It felt curly and it was in a style that I had not been familiar with. Boy, did I want his hair! As soon as I arrived home that day from school I pronounced to my mother that I wanted a haircut just like Kevin's. I was a little let down when my mom chuckled and tried to explain to me that my straight hair could never feel like his. Kevin Sparks was the first African American that I met. In high school he became an Indiana state wrestling champion. He was an example of hope, determination to excel, and inspiration for all-- especially those without physical impairments.

Blake in 1971

My first momentous learning milestone, taking place in the first grade, was learning Braille. I can still hear the assuring voice of my teacher, Mrs. Palmerlan, as she said, "Blake, let's learn some Braille today." For further encouragement, she told me the story *The Little Engine That Could*, a favorite among children and educators. I recall my brand new mentor telling me the best and most exciting part of the story, "I think I can, I think I can", roared the engine as it successfully made its way up over the high mountains. It was the first time I ever heard this confidence-boosting anecdote, and it certainly convinced me to exert my effort as I desired to resemble that positive powerful little engine. Somewhere deep inside, I knew that I could, too.

For the first few months, I was not a fan of Louis Braille, as Braille was difficult to learn and extremely challenging. The letter S resembled the letter P, but with one less dot on the top left. The letter M felt like N, but with one less dot on the right middle side. I was still having difficulty when entering my second grade year, but my main homeroom teacher, Mrs. Davidson, was a genuine, caring, encourager who had a true passion for Braille. She took time first of all to find out specifically which Braille letters were similar enough to frequently fool me. She would then put them side by side so that I could clearly feel and understand the difference between them. Finally, this out-of-the-ordinary code called Braille made sense. Mrs.

Davidson was successful in not only helping me to see her vision, but to also make her vision mine. Braille increased my independence just like she knew it would.

Mrs. Davidson

Dad used to tell us that, "'I Can,' is an attitude, 'I Will,' is an intent, 'I Am,' is taking action, and, 'I Am Glad I Did,' or, 'We're Glad We Did,' is nearly always the result." I can review my time and realize many challenges that I met head-on, like this important required challenge of learning Braille. Because of true teamwork, my mentor, Mrs. Davidson, and I can now pronounce, "We're glad we did."

Today, I often wonder how I could have survived in the world without knowing this remarkable system of communication. Braille has been a major contributor to my independence and I thank God for Louis Braille. He was not just an ordinary man; he was a visionary and quite simply… a genius! When people ask me who my heroes are, I quickly consider Louis Braille as a prime example.

On the subject of elementary school, blind kids are just like ordinary sighted kids in terms of what it is they like best, besides recess. My answer is quite simple: Field trips. I refer to the blind school field trips as "pure edutainment." Seldom have I heard this word used in people's conversations, however the unique expression appropriately defines our educational, entertaining field trips.

My favorite field trip was attending the Murat Shrine Circus in Indianapolis at the Pepsi Coliseum. Being guests of the Shriners permitted students from my school to have access to some special privileges not offered to others. I was glad for that because I finally got to meet an elephant. Not that I had been previously desiring to meet one, but it was nice to get a better picture of what it meant when Joy, my cousin, used to tease me about having an elephant's memory.

The elephant I had the pleasure of meeting greeted me with a big wet kiss on my hand. I guess I considered this a friendly gesture that conjured up feelings of safety and security because moments later I found myself taking my first elephant ride. It astounded me back then as it does today that an animal can weigh over three tons. Even more astonishing was visiting this elephant's three-week-old baby that weighed in at 500 pounds! I recall thinking, "Wow, that's more than three average-size adult humans." My elephant experience was the beginning of a new hobby, collecting elephant memorabilia. Today, my compilation consists of two elephant lamps, a doorstop, a pillow on our couch, a toothbrush holder in our bathroom, and probably way more than enough elephant figurines on display.

That day, I also learned that a trip to the circus is not complete until you meet the person known as the *Fattest Man in the World*. Before meeting this portly gentleman, I considered myself to be a big seven-year-old. After all, I was four feet, five inches tall weighing in at an incredible 70 pounds. When I met this unnamed gentleman, I wrapped my arms around one of his legs to gain a better understanding of his physical stature. This man stood six feet, three inches tall and weighed more than the three-week-old elephant I had met earlier in the day— 700 pounds! "I'm going to be bigger than you someday," I firmly shouted.

Weighing ten times more than this seven-year-old and being nearly two feet taller, this grand personality wailed with laughter. I only grew to one-quarter of his 700 pounds and I lack five inches in reaching his height. No wonder he found my comment so hilarious.

Many of those present that day were probably wondering how the blind kids knew what was happening during the circus performances. It was sheer generosity. The very familiar voice of a man by the name of Fred Heckman volunteered his narrative talent. Fred was the news director for the number one rated local Indianapolis radio station WIBC. He brought the circus to life for those of us who could not use our eyes to visualize the sensational acts. Indiana Bell Telephone graciously made all of this possible by providing us with headsets, which allowed us to hear Mr. Heckman without disturbing the other guests. He enabled us to have a greater understanding of how incredible a circus is and helped us to gain an appreciation and respect for the amount of time and energy that is required behind the scenes to prepare for such an enormous undertaking. No one missed a single act thanks to his kindness. He was extremely vivid and colorful. I can still remember his great voice and wonderful way of describing in detail, and with emotion, what he was seeing so we could witness as well. Were we spoiled or what?

Mr. Heckman passed away several years ago; however, his legacy lives on at WIBC for his impressive contribution of twenty-five years of dedicated service.

Only one field trip literally stunk, in a most unforgettable way. Boy Scout Troop Sixteen at the blind school piled in to the school bus and proceeded to the Indianapolis Sewage Treatment Plant. Wow, talk about clearing out my sinuses! This field trip did the trick quick. Seriously though, the knowledge we gained during that one-of-a-kind outing was very enlightening. A few minutes into our tour we were all listening intently to our guide as he gave us the details on the remarkable process by which they cleaned the mucky water and purified it enough to safely swim in. As we continued down the tour trail, I became even more fascinated when our guide informed us that the water was now actually clean enough for human consumption. I didn't particularly desire to partake; however, I realized that this sewage treatment plant was truly supportive to our conservation. The purification process was quite amazing.

We went on many educational tours to several places of interest such as the Governor's Mansion, a top rated television station, a grand tour of the Indy Five Hundred facilities, and the large Hostess Bakery. We even went to the local Indianapolis zoo and the art museum. In all places we were surrounded with visual aids to describe all of the fascinating animals and amazing creative artwork.

When I was in the fifth grade our class enjoyed an excursion to a large McDonald's Restaurant. Of course it was a preferred place to eat among our young group. We were appreciative when our willing McDonald's manager tour guide thoroughly explained their many daily responsibilities in operating our favorite fast pace eating-place. Our major highlight of this visit was touring the kitchen. Our ears and noses were tuned in to our most wanted food being prepared to meet the many McDonald's customers' orders. These fun, memorable field trips helped us to gain knowledge and awareness on several subjects. It really was Pure "Edutainment."

The majority of teachers at the blind school were sighted; however, during my fourth and fifth grade years my homeroom teacher was totally blind. Her name was Ms. Judy Whiteman and she was into her fifteenth year of teaching when I had the pleasure of becoming one of her students. While I enjoyed and learned from all my teachers at the school, this relatable educator provided an extra boost of inspiration. Ms. Whiteman acted as a "visual" aid and model of excellence in representing the adult life of a blind person. She was a wonderful listener and easily retained her students' attention. With such an impressive teaching career, she commanded respect and deserved nothing less. She possessed a special instinct for knowing which students were not focused. Needless to say, I never tried to pull the wool over Ms Whiteman's eyes. I preferred to avoid the embarrassment, plus I really liked her alert and observant style of managing a good classroom.

One of the most amazing facts about Ms. Whiteman was her ability to type on a regular typewriter. It was literally moving to be in the same room and hear this fine lady type at an amazingly rapid rate, way above average. Her confidence was contagious and throughout her thirty-six-year teaching career with the Indiana School for the Blind, Ms. Whiteman touched the lives of many appreciative students. She made me understand what it was like to be a true independent blind person, which encouraged me to strive for the same kind of success in life.

Although it is no longer allowed in some educational settings, Ms. Whiteman invited my entire class of 11 students to her home on a beautiful summer Saturday in August. Even though she lived seventy miles or more from where most of the students lived, 80% of our class showed up with extreme enthusiasm for yet another memory-making event. I sure heard my share of jokes pertaining to me being cheaper by the dozen, because our pleasurable gathering coincidentally fell right on my twelfth birthday. This made our get together extra special for me.

Ms. Whiteman's Brother, John, nine years her junior and also totally blind, joined us for our exciting reunion. I was happy he did, as I quickly learned how much we both equally loved talking about radio broadcasting. Our group got a kick out of John teasing his big sister on being a tough and demanding teacher. He was a sophomore in high school when she began her impressive education career. In addition to being each other's sibling, I could also observe their intimate and affirming friendship.

Our new friend John fit right in and none of us had any difficulty with our twenty-year age difference. John and I remain good friends today.

Knowing fried chicken would be a universal favorite, Ms. Whiteman took the liberty of ordering more than enough KFC so that she could devote her time and undivided attention to us. In celebration of our special get-together, she impressed us when she presented her homemade chocolate chip cake for our delicious dessert. We had a blast playing tunes on their turntable and getting caught up on the summer's happenings. Throughout our visit on that distinctive day, Ms. Whiteman had further shown us her exceptional independence by being a wonderful hostess. Additionally, she demonstrated her superior cooking skills for us as we pleasurably devoured that scrumptious homemade cake.

Even though our enjoyable occasion wasn't about me turning twelve, I can think of at least a dozen reasons that it was a great way to celebrate my birthday. Wonderful memories from this day are my life-lasting present. I never will forget this first-class visit away from school which was also our last class reunion so far.

At home and in school I liked to talk. This pastime inspired a love for speech and drama. I embraced every opportunity to be in the spotlight. Mrs. Reed oversaw the speech and drama department. Today I regard her as one of my early mentors. I hope that she realized how much she helped plant the growing seeds for my later development in radio broadcasting, which expanded throughout my high school and adult life.

Field trips and great teachers—what more could I have asked for? Answer: Extracurricular activities. Our primary competitive sports included wrestling, swimming, and track and field. Cheerleading was also proudly presented at our school. Our competitors were typically local private schools as well as all four neighboring blind schools located in our surrounding states-- Michigan, Kentucky, Ohio, and Illinois.

To this day, I believe that our blind and low vision cheerleaders provided the best motivation, and sounded better, than any school against which we would compete. We enjoyed the opportunities to visit our bordering blind schools and liked having their students travel our direction to join us for a weekend of vigorous competition with our spirited sports.

During my fourth year a bowling alley was installed for providing great entertainment. The majority of us had never experienced handling a bowling ball prior to our thrilling recreational progress. We were happy to have the right railings installed to assist us as they enabled us totally blind students to accurately line up, face those ten pens and to give that bowling ball our best aim down the lane. These special railings were not gutter protectors, so we could still give that gutter a good cleaning with the ball if we weren't alert. This was the real deal and many of us became pretty good at our fresh new hobby.

Only twice in my life have I enjoyed the thrill of bowling a perfect strike and I can sure say that it was "spare fun," pardon my pun. My top score is eighty-five and I admired a couple of totally blind people who scored around one hundred twenty.

Our brand new bowling alley also contained a true luxury which our school had previously exposed us to in only a few designated offices. The luxury I'm referring to is central air-conditioning. While this extravagance is a genuine necessity in the South, Indiana primarily benefits from air conditioning three or four months out of the entire year. We felt quite energized to have our cool indoor swimming pool and now a brand new breezy bowling alley to help us chill out through scorching summer days. I grinned and chuckled when I learned that central air was installed throughout all of the school buildings. The humor is that the noticeable improvement took place shortly after I had departed. Yes, I just about got to enjoy the full upgrade.

The school allowed us to join the junior high wrestling team as young as the fifth grade. I took advantage of this and remained on the squad through the eighth grade. However that was the conclusion of my association with our school sports. I am pleased that I learned the valuable importance of exercise through our blind school's junior high wrestling and physical education classes. I currently enjoy a daily workout to stay firm and fit in order to feel and remain as healthy as I am able to. I own a Schwin Airlume exercise bike my parents purchased as a healthy Christmas gift several years ago. Since my Dad and brother Brad were coaches, Bryce was in the military and Brock worked at a workout center, I sure do have good coaches on reinforcing how to do the best sit-ups, push-ups, and a few other good exercises including lifting weights.

I was grateful for my years at the Indiana School for the Blind and in fulfilling my duties as an ISB Rocket (our team name at the blind school), but as I became older and reached my teenage years, I realized that my adult life would not consist of me living in the mostly sightless environment that I was used to at the school. I knew in just a few short years I would be an adult and that it was important for me to be prepared to do well in a more typical setting. I also knew that my time to transition into the world of the employed would soon arrive.

I was ready to take the next big step – public school with sighted students. At the start of my junior year in high school I transitioned to a regular public high, Westfield Washington High School. I went from being a Rocket to being a Shamrock. My parents approved of and supported this new journey. My first task was learning the names of my new classmates. I was used to having 15 students in each grade at the blind school but in this new setting I had my first new challenge of trying to memorize ten times as many names and voices. I could observe how much the students appreciated me learning their names and they made me feel very welcome.

Several sighted students asked if I could teach them Braille. I gladly accepted this educational endeavor and I was successful in teaching quite a few of my brand new peers this unique method of reading and writing. I began by Brailing out the entire alphabet and spread it out enough for them to see the difference in each letter. They would sometimes print the letter below the Braille to speed up the learning process. I would then Braille numbers right below the alphabet.

One student especially stood out in the learning process— my friend Rick Watkins who was a smart but slightly below-average student. His deficiency was apparently due to a lack of interest in certain academics because Rick excelled remarkably with Braille in an incredibly short time. He ended up being my best and most excited student. After only a couple of weeks Rick took pride in learning the additional abbreviations that even I didn't personally master until my second year of learning this special code.

Braille doesn't resemble print in any way so I am still impressed when I think of Rick's achievement. This experience really helped me realize the truth about setting one's mind to something of interest and seeing one's goal through completion. I was not only pleased with Rick's victory but was also delighted I could actually teach him something significant.

My junior year in high school was probably the most rebellious. I desired to do well but enjoyed pleasing people. For whatever reasons I gravitated toward the entertaining group who were a little mischievous like Rick. I'm glad we weren't physically destructive. Rick was a terrific friend who proved by mastering Braille that he had real ambition; however, he was also as carefree as a person could be. We took an immediate liking to each other and had a ton of fun. I always sat next to Rick in English class just to hear what he would blurt out next. Our English teacher often reprimanded him but in that phase of my life I was humored by his attempt at comedy. I was pure proof that kids will be kids. Perhaps I should regret that we were not fully seizing the opportunity of learning all that we could. I have real admiration for the youth minority who can be attentive and engaged like a motivated learner should be.

Rick and I frequently hung out at Danny's Pizza, where he worked, to talk about life, socialize with other customers, and to take in all the mouth-watering aromas. He could sure throw together a tasty pizza. One day he brought me home to hang out with his mother. She was an apartment manager and took me around to observe what to expect in one bedroom apartments. I think she was hoping to talk me into choosing one of her apartments when the time came. I certainly would have, had I not moved to Austin, Texas soon after high school graduation.

Looking back on my magnificent challenge of school transition that I successfully conquered with plenty of teamwork, I'm grateful that my family supported me in following through. This move absolutely helped in preparing me to face the brand new challenges which often require us to step out of our comfort zones--something that is vital to do. I believe that my exclusive experiences in a regular public school environment proved to provide a positive and effective transition into the universal world of work. I also know now how very much I was granted an opportunity to challenge and inspire my public school mates; just as I have been blessed to be able to do in the common work place.

Chapter 4 Navigating Through Darkness

People often ask me which of my four senses is the most valuable. With no reservation I always reply my hearing because of my superior sense of echo, which helps me avoid running into people or things. I use the echoes to guide me in walking around a person or an object in my direct path and perceive when to accurately make a turn as if I could see. Only two limitations come to mind: One is that I cannot hear when there is a flight of stairs going down; however, I can usually feel a draft. The other is that an object has to be at least waist-high before I pick up an echo. At times this has caused me pain—literally. Take, for example, a dog's favorite thing to mark his spot on…yes, a fire hydrant. Fire hydrants hurt. I can't, for the life of me, figure out why dogs like them so much. I don't particularly care for their height or lack thereof. Fortunately though, if I am properly using my cane, I no longer deal with this dilemma.

Another frequent enquiry from people is regarding how I am able to navigate unfamiliar areas. The journey of navigating started with my mobility instructor, Pat Soja. He taught me the importance of focusing on my hearing to assist in my independence. Part of the training I received involved complete concentration on my keenly sharpened sense of hearing in order to line up with traffic and confidently cross busy intersections with stoplights.

After my freshman year in high school, something very exciting and life-changing happened. I experienced self-navigation in my home town. My family lived in the small suburb of Westfield, just north of Indianapolis. Mr. Soja patiently and effectively educated me with walking all over town. He first taught me how to get to my favorite hot spots, otherwise known as places to eat. First was the bakery. A pleasant woman who worked there was very enthusiastic when I mastered the trip unattended. She quickly became an encouraging friend.

Mr. Soja and I also strolled to the post office and other helpful places. There were occasional mishaps, forgetting where to make a turn, going too far, or not going far enough. Once I had down the ability to walk about freely, I had a great sense of independence. Through people's friendly communication, I sensed they were impressed and inspired watching me without a guide. Prior to learning self-navigation, I would often find myself with nothing to do and was restless. Suddenly, everything had changed for the better.

The following Christmas break I decided to take a walk. The only difference this time was the eight inches of snow on the ground. Snow is a bit of a hindrance for blind people because we rely primarily on sound to help us navigate. It resembles carpet, muting sound waves and surroundings to be silenced. An inch of snow mutes sound so you can imagine what big snowdrifts do. They create significant barriers and believe me when I tell you; they achieve this distraction in more ways than one.

I found out the hard way on that cold winter day as I was returning home from a solo walk. I became disoriented and missed my turn. Fortunately my mother knew my expected arrival time and when I didn't make it home, she went out to search for her aggressively independent son. She found me, took me home and thawed me out! I learned a great lesson about navigating after a snowstorm.

Today, I do not have to worry too much about traveling in the snow. Dallas, Texas, does not get wintry weather like Indiana. While snow has its amusing moments, I am grateful for southern weather patterns for mobility's sake.

Occasionally, I get disoriented when learning new territory. But if I learn the route I am taking with the assistance of a good traveler, I am able to memorize poles, shrubs, and other markings that I can feel or hear which helps me stay on track.

When it comes to traveling, a number of my blind friends choose to use seeing-eye dogs. These well-trained dogs can be a great guiding companion and a fun friend. These amazing animals expand visually impaired people's newfound freedom to the maximum. It is enjoyable to observe the increased confidence demonstrated by blind people, especially those who desired additional assurance. I have never felt a true need for a guide dog myself. For me, using a cane is the way to go. This subject is frequently addressed and I teasingly say to people that I have a stick dog named Bruiser and that he requires no food, water, potty breaks, or trips to the veterinarian.

I was introduced to my stick dog (walking cane) at age eleven when I took a mini-mobility course at the Indiana School for the Blind. On and off I enjoyed additional training and by age 15 I completely understood the importance of using the cane for my independence. I began to train quite intensely on mobility movements.

One of the most phenomenal things I have learned about all people is our God given ability to develop and sharpen our senses rather quickly. I have witnessed firsthand this rapid development of hearing through working with sighted mobility instructors.

Each person undergoing mobility instructor school is required to perform several times while blindfolded before they can earn their license to teach orientation mobility. In only a few days, without taking a break from wearing the blindfold, these people, as well as those who recently lose their eyesight, develop out of necessity the same expanded echo perception that I benefit from. The improvement of this "radar hearing" happens in only a few days. We would all be pleasantly surprised with the senses we can uncover and take advantage of when survival is our main concern.

I was a tour guide for the Indiana School for the Blind. Our tours often observed there were several incidences where we had to walk up and down flights of stairs to get from point A to point B. Someone in the group would usually ask, "How do you handle that many steps so well?"

My reply, while grinning, was, "One step at a time." Guests enjoyed that response.

I frequently teased tour groups by saying, "Don't think of me as blind, but instead think of me as a person who is out of sight." I usually had a smile on my face and I tried to maintain a good attitude. I wasn't perfect in that department but have always been happier than unhappy. I have observed that each of us, in one way or another, learns to adapt and compensate; whether it is for the loss of a faculty, being too short or tall, or having other special needs that are uncommon. Everybody is special in one way or another. We were terrifically and wonderfully made by Father God.

Chapter 5 Blind Boy Scouts

Sixteen was the official number of the Boy Scout troop of which I was a proud member for four years at the Indiana School for the Blind. We earned merit badges, went camping, learned to pitch tents, build fires to stay warm, cook over hot coals, and became familiar with outdoor survival techniques. We occasionally went to Boy Scout camp in the summer. I swam a quarter of a mile without stopping and earned badges I proudly displayed on my Boy Scout uniform.

My favorite boy scouting memories surround snow skiing trips to Merrimack, Wisconsin. Two winters in a row we traveled to Devil's Head Resort for three days of unforgettable snow skiing and winter vacation adventures. The snow skiing instructors were specially trained to teach blind people how to ski. I realize now, more than ever, how exceptional these instructors were. Their desire was to leave a thrilling memory for countless people who were blind. They were enthusiastic and confident as they took on this life-sized responsibility. They truly had a special gift for instilling their assurance in us, allowing us to boldly zip down huge hills covered in soft white blankets of snow. Our instructors would stay five or so yards behind us as we skied down the hills so they could effectively shout orders to turn right or left in plenty of required time. We also learned the importance of crashing right or left upon demand, which simply means to fall down at once to the right or left. Crashing was the quickest and easiest way to stop in order to avoid appending danger. I only had one close call involving a potential collision with another skier who probably didn't know I was blind. Needless to say, I sure didn't see the skier. No calamity occurred because I listened attentively to the commands of my alert instructor. Thank goodness I knew that he was a leader who I could believe in for superior safety.

On many occasions I have been asked to speak to groups of people specifically on the theme of top performance leadership. I'm delighted to have my own significant example to share with you because it completely illustrates competent, caring, difference-making leadership at its very best. Without my superb ski instructor who demonstrated such leadership, I absolutely could not have made this exhilarating snow skiing memory.

A life lesson learned is how valuable teachers, coaches, and leaders are to our personal and professional development. It is a thrill today for me to be able to give back to others by being a teacher, coach, or mentor in sharing my know-how with others. It is both an honor and a duty for us to share knowledge, skills, and life insights with those seeking our coaching, mentoring, or counsel.

Chapter 6 Blake and His Cycles

From the days of my sister pulling me around on her tricycle with me behind on my roller skates, I thrived on the independence I felt when soaring on two wheels. That same fascination continued into the spring of my second grade year when Dad proudly accommodated my request to remove the training wheels from my bike.

To ensure a painless experience, I first learned how to ride a bicycle in the front yard with Mom and Dad walking beside me. Once I was confident riding in our front yard, Dad bought a nice two-seated bike, called a tandem, from a retired couple right before my ninth birthday. This enabled me to learn to ride on the street. My parents were very pleased that a blind boy and his dad would enjoy the bike while having plenty of quality dialogue along the way. It had three technical meters including a speedometer, tachometer, and an odometer which had only twenty miles registered.

A couple of times each week during the summer and early fall, Dad and I rode in tandem on a six-mile journey. The ride took us approximately thirty-six minutes to complete as we averaged ten miles an hour. Throughout the last couple of minutes of our ride we opened up and traveled at our top speed of twenty-five miles per hour, resembling an eager horse running for the barn after a vigorous day's work.

Dad's legs were much quicker than mine. So if we happened to speed up to around twenty-eight miles an hour, I took the liberty of enjoying a Blake break until he slowed down to twenty-five, where I could keep up again. It was exciting maintaining the momentum with a motorized vehicle driving along a residential street. I hoped the person driving observed our fast pace and was as thrilled as I was with our energetic team effort.

The next spring, a few months before my tenth birthday, Dad surprised me with this abnormal action. He put my hand on the single bike which I often rode in our yard and asked if I would like to follow him on nearby residential streets, trailing close behind him. I was reluctant but decided to give this a try. I got right behind him and heard him peddling. When he wasn't peddling he would talk to me so

I could stay lined up with him. Initially I encountered a few accidents but became better and more confident each ride.

I quickly learned to stay in Dad's direct path or else I would experience the discomfort of an unpleasant ouch from running into a mailbox, street sign, or curb. I had complete faith my Dad would alert me to anything unknown which could pose a problem. He trusted I would follow his navigational lead from his voice and bike noise. If Dad ran over a small object, such as a paper cup someone had previously thrown on to our path, I was then able to steer the exact pathway and my two wheels would literally roll over the same litter. I was now more at ease than ever and gained great assurance knowing Dad was leading the way a few feet ahead of me. True victory came when we were able to travel around town with me on my own bike. It was especially exciting when someone occasionally assumed I was my sighted older sibling, Brad, riding along with Dad. They would say "Hi Brad."

I would turn to them with a big happy grin and say, "Hi, I'm Blake." Since they knew I had no sight I imagine they thought that was genuine father and son adventure.

Dad and I haven't lived close enough to consistently ride together for more than two decades. After our more than twenty-year hiatus, Dad surprisingly suggested that we take this challenging and enjoyable kind of bike ride again. I was a little off the beaten path at first but within a few short minutes I was enjoying an incredibly fun time like before. I'm especially relieved that I have no accident to report because I don't believe I am nearly as limber as I was twenty-plus years ago.

During one ride a friendly neighbor and Sunday school teacher, Dorotha Mack, was riding her bicycle and saw me following Dad in complete trust. I had never met her before and she turned to me and said with total interest and passion, "Wow! You're doing great!"

A couple of weeks later during a telephone visit with my mother, Dorotha eagerly mentioned that it was very uplifting to her as she was going through a down time. I was thrilled to hear Dorotha was inspired by our demonstration of trust and that it had reinforced how we should respond to our Heavenly Father.

Most people, myself included, would probably think that my Dad should have been satisfied with us riding together in our stress-free comfort zone on the tandem bicycle; however, when I heard

Dorotha's awesome observation, it became obvious to me that God had simply looked ahead and knew that we had some inspiring to do.

Just like my skiing experience, Dad demonstrated the huge impact one person can have on another who is willing to listen, believe, and obey wise guidance and coaching. This is also the kind of trust we should have in our Lord so that we can enjoy the best quality and most productive results in our lives. I also made a brand new, priceless friend named Doratha Mack because of this awesome event.

A few days before the start of my sophomore year of high school, I turned 16. As with any other 16-year-old, I fantasized about what it would be like to get my driver's license. This was a situation where I had the vision but not the sight. I accepted this reality and I dealt with it.

Three weeks before my senior year of high school my parents and siblings moved to the Dallas/Fort Worth, Texas, area. I chose not to transition with my family, as I wanted to finish my high school education with my friends and teachers at my hometown public school. I felt it was too soon for me to adjust once and it was nearly time to graduate. It was also my second year working at the ice skating facility, providing me additional independence with a decent amount of spending money. Thanks to my mother's parents, I moved in with them which allowed me to graduate with my class. And even better providing the opportunity for us to become closer. I am thankful for this unexpected quality time with them.

Blake, Mam, and Pap

Mam and Pap were kind and loving grandparents who had been married for more than 50 years and were a wonderful team throughout Pap's lengthy pastoral tenure. Nearly everyone in town knew them and was extremely fond of them. Pap was a senior pastor at Westfield Friends Church for ten fulfilling years, and they made this town their home through the majority of their retirement.

Both of my grandparents took an active part in helping my senior year go smoothly. My grandmother took care of my stomach with her great home cooking and my grandfather took care of my mobility instruction. Pap was very perceptive and helpful with orientation to my new surroundings. He had a true knack for introducing me to good landmarks such as shrubs, poles, and other permanent structures to feel or listen for. Before long I was thrilled to be back in the business of traveling independently and, once again, expanding my horizons by roaming where I had never walked alone before.

My grandfather was almost 77 years old, yet he got a kick out of the numerous times I encouraged him to forget about retirement and begin a brand new career of teaching mobility orientation to the blind. When my grandparents kindly took on the responsibility of being my guardians throughout my senior year, I believe that neither of them had any clue what I was going to put them through. It certainly wasn't my goal to put them through anything but I was, without a doubt, a blind, adventurous teenager and preparing to prove it more than ever.

A couple of weeks after I moved in with my grandparents, I got together with my good friend Brian Belter. Brian used to spend his money recklessly as he was an impulsive buyer who quickly became bored with some of his larger purchases. He offered me a bargain on something I always dreamed of owning. I was so excited about his good deal, it was incredibly easy for me to choose not to refuse – and I bought Brian's two-month-old Honda MB5 motorcycle.

Yes, Blind Blake bought a motorcycle! I did not ask for anyone's permission or blessing for that purchase knowing that there would be none. My grandparents were indeed surprised and extremely nervous. I assured them time and time again that I would be careful with my compact 198-pound bike. I had more confidence riding on a smaller bike as opposed to the normal sized three-to-four-hundred-fifty pound motorcycles. Experience taught me that the bigger bikes are obviously more difficult to hold up if they happen to accidentally tip over. Fortunately it only took one time for me to learn that lesson, and thank goodness I didn't fall all of the way over.

On my motorcycle at age 18 in October of 1982. It was hard to part with such a thrilling ride, and it sure beat walking!

My treasured new vehicle was great on gas and plenty fast for quick trips around town with my fearless friends. The engine was equipped with seven horsepower, which was just enough muscle to push us to a top speed of 60 miles per hour. However, we seldom went above forty in town.

My friends took me on rides and escorted me to open parking lots and long sidewalks where I could ride solo. They made certain I was in the clear for a good clean ride with no obstacles. I was very proud of purchasing my motorcycle and took great care of it - washing and polishing it by myself to keep it looking mint.

One day I was happily zipping down the sidewalk on my Honda. Yes, I was alone and riding my speedster around twenty miles an hour down the sidewalk. In the background I heard a police siren. As the sound became closer I suspected it was specifically meant for me, so I stopped.

The police officer questioned the ownership of the bike and I politely informed him I was indeed the owner. He then proceeded to explain that if he saw me on the bike zipping down a sidewalk again, he would impound it immediately. I had never met the officer before, however he must have known that I was without sight. I suspected he had seen me walking around town alone with my stick dog/cane Bruiser, as I had two full years of walking freedom at this point.

The police officer wanted to instill the danger of me unexpectedly running into something or somebody. I explained to him that I had walked the "rough" in advance, making certain that no toys such as Big Wheels, bikes, or other toys were in my path. But I knew he was right on. There is always the unexpected. I can only imagine what that officer was thinking when he pulled over a blind teenager riding a motorized vehicle. What a unique comical hoot he probably enjoyed sharing with his colleagues!

I was appreciative that I received a good strong warning, as opposed to the money-devouring ticket I could have incurred. I was also grateful that I never had any major incidences while riding, with the exception of scraping my hand on a mailbox.

At the time, Westfield had approximately 3,200 residents. I was in my second year of hometown public school and many of my fellow students talked about me often. Most of our town applauded the blind Lindsay boy, mostly due to my fearless freedom getting around town by myself. My parents were plenty proactive in introducing me to our fellow church and school members. The townsfolk may have been comforted when the bike and the blind rider moved out of town, as upon my move to Texas I sold my motorcycle. Good chance many Texans were unknowingly grateful for this. I still dream about my exciting experience of actually owning my own motorcycle all of these years later.

Mam and Pap were plenty relieved when I graduated from high school free of any major mishaps while I lived with them. I love them and will never forget what they did for me during my senior year. Mam lived about twelve more years, to age 85, and Pap lived to nearly 99. If I'm blessed to live that long, I bet that I'll even be boasting about those bonus half years. So, I enjoy bragging about Pap's long life span.

For several years after I moved out of their home, Pap and I enjoyed re-visiting our memorable mobility-bonding along with our unexpected motorcycle adventure. What an interesting year we both had.

Chapter 7 Blake Goes to Camp

The excitement and anticipation of attending summer camp can be heard in the voices of elementary aged children at the close of a school year. For this sightless child, the thrill of attending summer camp was just as real. Camp Timber Ridge offered a week of fun for children who were blind or with low vision. Several weeks in advance my parents built my excitement as they discussed with me the idea of attending camp. I enjoyed them sharing their personal stories of staying in cabins and all the excitement that summer camp had offered. They sent me packing with an overwhelming desire to take in all I could while camping.

The landscape surrounding the site was filled with rolling hills and a wide variety of trees. In the mornings, the air would have that wonderful freshness about it. It smelled crisp and invigorating. It made me envision what heaven could be like, especially after a good rain when the world smelled alive and happy.

At the campground I soon discovered the sassafras, an aromatic tree that can reach heights of over 60 feet. It was a treat to chew on the stems of its leaves. This native delicacy was like enjoying the refreshing taste of breath mints. I had always liked peppermints and cinnamon balls but had never had the real thing before these stems and leaves get transformed into candy. The long refreshing taste of this natural spice right from the tree was like nothing I had ever tasted before.

At camp, I rode horses and was taught to shoot an arrow at a target with the help of excellent archery instructors. I loved swimming in the big, clean lake, riding on speedboats, and zip sledding behind the watercraft. At night we gathered around the campfire to sing songs and tell scary stories.

On the evening before going home, there was a talent show in which I eagerly participated. I played *America the Beautiful* on a harmonica my mom and dad had purchased for me. It was a nice-looking instrument and I had become polished at playing the song.

From that point forward, Camp Timber Ridge became a part of my summer ritual. I gladly participated four more times. With my parents' encouragement, I performed in three subsequent talent shows, playing the piano with pride. They taught me the importance of sharing the talents God is lending me here while on earth. I'm happy they encouraged me in music.

Here I am riding atop an awesome horse at summer camp in July of 1975. I enjoyed the days I spent at Camp Timber Ridge.

Chapter 8 Summer School Memories

Reflecting on some of the most enjoyable summers in my young life, they included camp and summer school for the blind. Summer school was four, fun-filled, optional weeks without the pressures of academics or tests. It was with a smaller group of around 40 students ranging from fifth grade through high school. We had a blast, behaving like one big family, as we enjoyed this relaxed environment with expanded opportunities to become acquainted with each other. The teachers valued the added month of income and we appreciated getting to expand our horizons.

It was recommended that I take orientation mobility during several sessions to introduce to me to the importance of using a cane. I am grateful that I had a head start on learning to properly use this mobility device at age eleven. An early feeling of independence would be my priceless reward.

Eating has always been a favorite thing for me to do. I love to eat good, home-cooked food, and I also enjoy eating at good restaurants. I was certainly happy that home economics was offered during the summer months to help me gain a sense of confidence and independence, along with a couple of extra pounds. During class time, I learned to scramble eggs, grill cheese sandwiches, bake cookies from scratch, and whip up batches of delicious homemade potato chips. Thank goodness those flavorful, fattening foods didn't become the greater portion of my permanent diet. In addition to learning how to cook with electronic appliances, Mrs. Lobdell taught us how to sew and clean. Vacuuming with an electric sweeper was one of my personal favorites. I enjoyed hearing the sound of dirt or accidentally dropped crumbs being swept away, knowing that I was productively doing some good cleaning. Our home economics teacher would walk us through each cooking and cleaning project, mentioning helpful sounds to listen for along with things to feel for. We learned how to use measuring cups and other aids. Many cooking devices are now adapted for the blind with Braille or feelable markings. When I fill up a cup, I am using my hearing for the pitch along with occasionally feeling the weight which also shows me exactly how full the glass is. Quite honestly, just like tying a shoe, I don't think about how I do many things until I am asked to give examples. It's humorous to me that only then do I have to think about how I accomplish certain tasks. I undoubtedly admire teachers for their trained ability to break the learning process down and detail each step. With sewing, I never got great at threading the needle but was pretty good at staying in a straight line. I even made a small pillow or teddy bear when I was nine years old in art class at the Blind School. We would feel how our teacher was doing it first and would be well supervised during our projects. I was glad for smaller sized classes at the Blind School for the best one-on-one teaching.

Our summer school field trips included visiting the Indianapolis Indians to watch a few games and journeying to Conner Prairie Farms to gain a better mental and physical perspective on how people lived and bartered during the 1800's. Another highlight of recreational summer school was learning to play miniature golf. I never got great but enjoyed the teachers lining me up and applauding when I struck the ball as they had taught me. They showed me how to hold the golf club and how it should feel to correctly swing it for the best results.

We also took overnight trips to different countrysides, learning the diverse Indiana terrain. We also engaged in stimulating sports competition playing kickball and when we were indoors in the gym, we enjoyed playing ground volleyball. I would listen and know where everyone was and find out where the ball needed to travel in an effort to score a home run. I would place the ball in front of my right foot and then kick that ball for all I was worth. One day we were playing kickball during the summer going into my eighth grade year. I was so excited when I scored a home run that I stood at home plate for a few too many seconds. Out of nowhere I was plowed over by one of my older and bigger teammates, Jerry, as he was running for home. Because of the extra boost of adrenalin that was running through my body, falling back onto my left pinky didn't even hurt at first. To my dismay, my smallest finger quickly became my largest as it swelled bigger than my thumb. This was the first major injury I had sustained in my life. It turned out I broke my finger in two

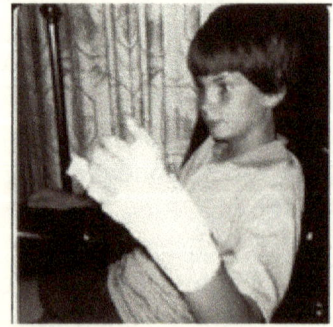

This is a result of making a mouth-dropping home run during a friendly game of kick ball. Even though I loved the attention, I couldn't wait to have that plaster cast removed.

places. Even though I was injured, I was also excited. Now I was finally wearing the kind of cast most boys love to show off at some point in their lives—and I was no exception.

At first I loved the attention and buzz my new 'armband' created. By the third week, however, I was happy to have the cast removed so I could return to the joys of swimming, bathing, and playing sports. I was relieved the accident happened when it did or I would have missed my first water skiing experience three weeks prior. Luckily it didn't occur until a month and a half later when I was returning to the regular academic school year. The cast happened to be on my precise hand I use to read Braille. I learned a lesson then which expanded my gratitude forever. That nothing beats having the use of both your hands, a reality that I will never again take for granted.

Chapter 9 Music Man

At the young age of four I was motivated by music. Such as the song *Feeling Groovy* by Harpers Bizarre, an upbeat tune with positive lyrics that quickly grabbed my attention. It would make me smile all day as I heard it playing over and over again in my mind.

My grandparents had an old upright piano and I learned to peck out melodies like Chopsticks, Peter Peter Pumpkin Eater, and several others. I took more and more interest in forming real chords and melodies. I was able to hear the tunes in my mind and then feel around until I found the right keys to duplicate those melodies. It was also fun and challenging to teach myself the melodies that my relatives were playing on the piano.

Soon after my eighth birthday, my parents found a talented piano teacher experienced in teaching people who were sighted and blind. She was completely sighted; however, she knew how to teach Braille music. This was a genuine bonus for me as well as her two sightless students before me. Coincidently, Mrs. Moxley and I shared the same birthday. She was a skilled pro – in fact a concert pianist. She had complete confidence without arrogance.

Mrs. Moxley was not only a terrific keyboard player but she also had a voice that could complete an incredible four-octave range. Her angelic sound was music to my ears. Born in 1918, she was an awesome storyteller and she often talked about her childhood. For instance, her family owned and operated the large, well-known Ball jar manufacturing company in Muncie Indiana. It was fascinating to me that the familiar Ball State University was named in honor of her family.

Lucina Hall, a dormitory at Ball State University, was named in the honor of my teacher, Lucina Ball Moxley. She was a fairly wealthy lady whose motivation wasn't driven by her students' financial compensation. She fervently shared her musical delight with her students. Mrs. Moxley hoped that her contagious enthusiasm would help me develop into a musician. She had elevated expectations for each pupil. I was fond of my teacher; however, I didn't always enjoy those challenging one-hour lessons. She was a real taskmaster and wanted to take advantage of every second of the practice. My wonderful mother was determined to keep me encouraged and she proved it by putting forth plenty of her loving effort. She considerately brought me a soda to help get me fired up for a good session and she nearly always made one of my favorite meals to precede my piano lesson. Mother was devoted to developing my talent. She gave her undivided attention as she supervised my piano practices four or five nights each week. She patiently taught me several songs assigned to me by my mentor. Knowing my passion for music, my parents surprised me with the gift of a spinet piano just five months into my lessons. When relatives or friends came over I had a captive live audience. If they twisted my arm a little I played several songs for them. My audience always made me glad that I accommodated their requests. Mrs. Moxley mentored me for six years and she was truly a caring, competent, difference-making leader who I think of often.

The piano is one of several musical instruments I play. At the Indiana School for the Blind, Mr. Porter, my band director, taught me to play the clarinet and saxophone. He had been a band director in public schools but he had developed a unique knack for teaching blind people just as well. He taught me to carefully hold the instrument and then he placed my fingers right on the right keys to make the notes. We were both equally determined on this one. He thoroughly enjoyed coaching and encouraging us to improve with our music making. He was into his eighth year when I joined band.

We loved entering band contests and competing against other schools with sighted students. This was quite inspiring not only to me, but also to those sighted people against whom we were competing. Because of my band director's first-rate coaching, I proudly brought home several first place medals.

Our school for the blind also had an outstanding chorus under the guidance of Mrs. Price, another example of a superior leader. We showed off our talents on the stage by performing at our annual Christmas concerts. We even took the stage in downtown Indianapolis on the monument circle right before Christmas. We were proud to quickly attract a live, cheering audience. People were drawn because our songs blasted through a high quality sound system provided by the city. Our chorus put on musicals and plays such as *Oliver Twist*. We also provided the entertainment for our high school graduation ceremonies.

When I transitioned from the Indiana School for the Blind to my hometown public school, Westfield Washington High School, I joined the marching band. Mr. Krum, the high school band director, assigned me to the percussion section. I had the unique opportunity of carrying the school flag during our high school parades. Fortunately, I had a person on each side of me who would politely give me a nudge to keep me in a straight line.

I must admit my musical talents were more appropriately used during basketball games when our pep band, not a marching band, rose on the stands and rallied our team with blasts of music. I felt right at home being stationary and playing the familiar tenor saxophone.

One evening I went to the mall with some family friends, Ruby and Ted Whitmoyer, who knew I could play the piano. They casually took me into a piano store in the middle of the mall, sat me down on the bench of a brand new grand piano, an item that costs thousands of dollars, and requested that I play a song. I obliged. Before long, an audience stood around the piano. The salesman teasingly asked me if I was out to get his job. I assured him not to be too concerned, as I was fifteen and not seeking employment at the time. I should admit I was somewhat hopeful I could help him sell one of those luxurious pianos. And he might generously throw a twenty dollar bill in my pocket so I could freely spend it in the mall. But we were there only a few minutes and it didn't happen.

I have always loved music and was often blessed to play the piano at various church services and banquets. With the help from my mentors I play the keyboard, clarinet, saxophone, and light percussion. Though I enjoy music and all it has to offer, I never really had the desire to make it a profession. This slightly disappointed my parents. I got a kick out of teasing my wonderful Mom and Dad about how they could have had a son who was a famous blind musician just like the parents of Stevie Wonder, Ray Charles, and Jose Feliciano.

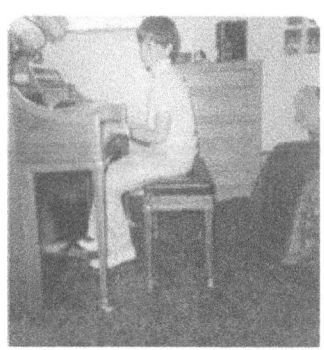

At the helm of a piano, which I played for hours as a child.

My parents still desire me to share my music at church and civic activities. This is something I have recently taken seriously and I enjoy performing now much more than I did during my younger years. I am more carefree about playing and not as concerned about accidentally missing a note. I just give it my best shot. The piano has traveled with me from Indiana to Texas and now is set up in my living room, allowing me the opportunity to play anytime I want.

Chapter 10 Blake the Swimmer

The summer following first grade my family drove to my Aunt Joan and Uncle Jim Vogel's house in Knights Town, Indiana. The 90 mile round trip adventure was an enjoyable journey we took several times every summer. I was always excited about making the one-hour trip each way, as I got to spend quality time with my aunt, uncle, and three cousins. Their caring and inspiring personalities really made them a fun family.

This particular trip had a forever lasting impact on my life. Memorial Day weekend marked the official pool opening at the Vogel home. The water was usually chilly and positively exhilarating. However, the temperature of the water was just right on this particular holiday. I officially became a swimmer. No more supportive vest, no more sinking—just full-blown, dog-paddling swimming. This triumphant experience took place about three months away from my seventh birthday. The year before, I had transitioned from an inner tube to a vest that barely held me above the water. Aunt Joan bought me this special vest after watching another little boy using one in her pool. She thought I should have it as the vest would make me have to work harder to stay afloat. It truly did the trick as I had to learn to propel myself. Swimming was only a little more difficult without the vest but the thrill of independence this event brought me was amazing. I get a grin on my face when I think back on this special day as Aunt Joan's applauds and cheers still echo in my mind. Imagine how this six-year-old boy squealed with excitement when we frequently returned to my aunt and uncle's house that same summer to celebrate school's summer break.

Dad noticed me frequently jumping off of the side of the swimming pool and told me how much more fun it would be to leap off of the diving board. I was aware that the board was three feet above the nine foot deep water. The thought of jumping off of it was frightening. Dad brought over a sturdy chair for me to jump from and coached me into jumping from it. I enjoyed the extra fun provided from the added height and gained the confidence to jump off the diving board. Dad pulled the chair over to the diving board, took my hand, and let me feel for myself what he saw. There was only about a foot contrast from the height of the chair and the top of the diving board. I worked up some courage from Dad's coaching and reluctantly jumped off the board. Wow! What a thrill! Immediately realizing how much fun I had just enjoyed, you couldn't keep me away from repeatedly leaping off the diving board. I loved the time I spent in the pool with my terrific relatives.

Following the successful swimming adventure, my family vacationed at Duarte Lake in Northern Indiana. The lake had a high diving board, provided a vast amount of space for swimming, and a brand new aroma--which I enjoyed. It was great. But what would a visit to a lake be without a boat ride? Fortunately that was a question I never had to answer. The opportunity to ride in a boat came upon me and I could not wait. To my surprise, the vessel I would ride in was not a pontoon boat but an actual speedboat. I remember my first exciting experience of smelling the boat's gasoline-powered engine and putting my hand on the top of the water as we sped along. I fantasized about how great it would be if I could swim as fast as this boat was carrying me across the water.

A year later my family traveled to Louisville, Kentucky for a five-day vacation. During this trip seven-year-old Blake experienced the feeling of free falling. Yes, I took to the real high dive. My parents got me all excited reading the brochure of where we were vacationing and about a high diving board. I never will forget counting each step and excitedly reaching the diving board. I centered myself by carefully walking down the board until the tips of my toes were touching the end. Standing 12 feet above the water and completely fearless, I leaped into the air. My body tingled as I sensed my momentum gaining. With great excitement I made that fearless jump more than a dozen times and certainly didn't realize that my high diving event was getting ready to abruptly end.

The adults and kids that were watching me began to tell me how brave I was for jumping at such a dangerous height. Many stated they would never do what I was doing and that if I could actually see how high I was on that diving board that I wouldn't either. They were sowing fear into my life. They thought they were complimenting me but as I heard how daring it was, doubt and fear completely consumed my thoughts. So as I began the much slower climb up the high dive stairs for another flight from the diving board, I became utterly cautious. I carefully counted each step on this ladder, which now seemed as tall as Mount Everest. When I finally reached the top, I started to panic as the words of the spectators replayed in my mind. I crept forward on the diving board at a snail's pace. When my toes felt the end where I had so excitedly leaped off before, terror literally took over as I froze on the edge of the board teetering out over the water.

Dad told me not to be afraid and that it was not an option for me to back-down now. He wanted me to face my fear and stand it down, but I was scared. Dad could be kind and stern, and also commanding and stern. Well, this time he commanded me to face this unnecessary fear. After all, I had done it so many times before fright abruptly took a bight from my previous delight. He was simply trying to teach me the power of negative words and they can cause us to miss out on some exciting episodes of our lives if we allow them to take root. Dad knew that I could make the jump at least one more time. He also knew "God does not give us a spirit of fear, but of love, power, and a sound mind" (I Timothy 1:7).

To give everyone my best effort in proving I was still a big boy, with eyes wide open I finally jumped off. Not once, but twice for good measure, following my needlessly fearful experience. God tells us in so many places that we should be strong and courageous, knowing that he is always there.

I learned a positive, valuable lesson from this escapade – it's funny how people can infuse fear in others even when there is nothing to be afraid of. This is what my dad was trying to tell me that day by having me continue my jump just as I had enjoyed doing all day long. It would still be several years before I would tackle the high dive again.

Today I appreciate the fact that Dad did not want me to become the victim of the onlookers' unnecessary remarks, and the doubt and fear they put into my mind.

I conquered the pool and a lake, and now I was about to get the opportunity to conquer something even bigger…the ocean! My Aunt Joan and Aunt Nancy invited Brad and me to take our first trip to Florida with them. Our parents had recently acquired additional responsibility with my baby brother, Bryce, as he was only eleven days old at this point. So Mom and Dad were plenty busy and unfortunately couldn't join us.

Because of the many lifetime memories we made on this trip, I'm thankful that my parents let us travel without their parental supervision. For the first time in my life, I experienced the ocean and all it had to offer. Walking on the sandy beach and smelling the aroma of salt, I took deep breaths and soaked in the smell to my forever memory. I enjoyed the fragrance of the pool and lake, but the rich scent of the Atlantic Ocean quickly became my favorite. I purposefully tasted the salt water. I am sure that most kids are eager to try it when experiencing the ocean for the first time. For that matter, adults probably purposefully taste the water, too. Ocean waves are amazing and breathtaking.

My aunt provided us with a raft so that I could really experience the power and the rush of waves. My cousins joined me the first couple of times so I could understand how to listen for the wave and prepare the raft for taking me on a thrilling ride back to shore. There my aunt was waiting for my pleasurable response. Before long I was riding the waves in by myself. Then, as quickly as possible, swimming right back out to ride those amazing waves back in again. Wow! What a flurry of exhilarating entertainment I enjoyed for hours.

Years later, at the age of nearly fourteen, I joined my father's two brothers, Uncle Jim and Uncle Jack, for another water adventure. When I was younger I was taught to swim in a pool, taken for speedboat ride, and raft surfed in the ocean. And now there was a new challenge on the horizon - water skiing. This unforgettable adventure happened at Morse Reservoir in Central Indiana during the Fourth of July weekend. My two uncles and a handful of cousins witnessed my first water skiing experience. My Uncle Jim's big voice bellowed, "Blake, it's your turn. Are you ready?" I do not know if I was truly ready, but I trusted my family to make sure that my attempt at water skiing would be safe and secure.

I felt the powerful pull as the strong sturdy boat took off. I hadn't imagined the speedboat would have so much force, and I only held on for about five seconds before letting go. Uncle Jim laughed and blurted out, "Blake, you've got to hang on if you want to get up on those skis." By the third try, I had it down and loved the feeling of the wind in my face, water under my skis, and the force of the pulling. I'm thankful for Uncle Jim's patience as I found the courage to stand up on the water skis. And as you probably guessed, I am glad I did.

It was so much fun having that powerful motorboat pull me along the top of the water. Boats of all kinds have always fascinated me and they still do. As a child I had often heard people talking about water skiing and the thrill they received from doing it. Although I had some clues of what to expect, the actual thrill of really water skiing is almost beyond description. Oh boy was the memory ever alive the next morning as my arms screamed out in soreness. But what do they say? "No pain, no gain." My gain in accomplishing another first in my young life lives with me today.

Chapter 11 God's Protection

During my kindergarten year at the Indiana School for the Blind, my mother drove me to and from school nearly every day. Sometimes on our way home she would stop by the grocery store to purchase items needed for the preparation of that evening's meal. It was easier and quicker for Mom to have me wait in the car a couple of minutes. She typically returned in a fast five minutes.

One afternoon I stubbornly sought to join her in the store. I had slightly opened my door to join her when Mom quickly returned to the car. As she got in I forgot all about my passenger door being ajar. The door was not open wide enough to activate the ceiling light to alert my mother so off we drove. As the car approached the busiest intersection at rush hour, Mom made her usual left turn. The passenger door flew open and I, along with my cherished Winnie the Pooh, tumbled right out of the car into that busy intersection. There was no pain. Only the feeling of falling onto the street combined with the fear that my mother might not have seen me fall, leaving me prey to approaching vehicles. I could hear the traffic all around Pooh and me.

Of course my mother saw me fly out of the car. She was in shock as if it happened in slow motion. She immediately stopped and jumped out of the car. With no concern to any injury, my fear was that I had lost my Winnie the Pooh. "Don't worry, I have him," Mom calmly assured me. There was an immense sound of relief in her voice when she realized her little boy escaped the fall with no visible injuries. We got back in the car and Mom put Winnie back in my lap. Then we drove on home. This is not one of my mother's cherished memories.

My parents are Christians, and God's protection over the family is regularly asked for in prayer. Our Heavenly Father's shield of protection was certainly with Mom and me during that drive. As an adult reflecting on this event with my mother, we both realize how fortunate we were not to have been physically injured. My mom still gets a little embarrassed that I fell out of the car while she was driving over 30 years ago.

Needless to say, I learned my lesson regarding the use of seatbelts. And why cars and safety laws have been enhanced since then with the addition of car seats, child safety locks, and seatbelt laws. Today, I still make sure my door is completely closed when riding in someone's vehicle. As they say, "An ounce of prevention is worth a pound of cure."

Dad has often told another testimony of God's protection which took place when I was six years old. He was the athletic director and varsity basketball coach and later became the high school principal in our hometown. Dad took my brother, Brad, and me to the gymnasium at Westfield Washington's former high school. The newer gym where we usually played was occupied so Dad took us to the old gym. My brother played basketball while I found other things to do in the wide-open space.

Independent as I was, I decided to explore and climbed a fire escape attached to another part of the old school building. What I didn't know was this particular part of the school burned in a fire some time earlier. It was a dual stairway and fire escape. Right at the top and toward the left, the staircase ended without any protective handrail. It was wide open and I was making my way right in that direction, approximately 30 feet above a concrete parking lot. At the split second, Dad looked up to see me walking toward the end of the landing. I was less than a foot away from the edge when Dad shouted in an authoritarian voice emanating impending danger, "Blake, freeze!"

From the inflection in his voice I knew he was not joking and I stopped. He then calmly coached me to take two small steps backward and sit down. I obeyed without hesitation. Dad quickly ran up the fire escape to me.

This event reinforces my belief in the Holy Spirit's protection as my dad was inspired to look up at just the right time. It also taught me that even as children know their father's voice, we are spiritually believers in God and can know his voice through others.

Here's another answered prayer that took place nearly three months before I became a teenager. It positively affected our entire family and will always be a part of our testimony of God's grace, mercy, and protection. When school closed for our summer vacation, we all piled into our little Volkswagen bus, which comfortably seated seven and had plenty of room for our luggage. My parents had just purchased the vehicle and we were extra eager to take the first family vacation in it. Our technician friend Bob installed a CB radio antenna high atop the driver's side in case we required emergency assistance along the way. This also minimized any potential withdrawals from being absent from my home CB radio. This was my newest leading hobby and I liked the idea of taking a six-day vacation as long as it wasn't away from my CB radio. Dad drove us to Copper Mountain, Colorado, for an extended vacation. This made our vacation trip especially exciting as we had never been high up into the Rocky Mountains before. Friends of my father, Jerry and Sylvia DeWitt, owned a comfortable condominium at Copper Mountain and arranged for us to use it to celebrate Dad's completion of his doctoral dissertation at Ball State University.

Copper Mountain is close to Vail and Breckenridge, high up in the Rockies to make it extra appealing and adventurous for Brad, Molly, and me. This particular vacation continues to bring back wonderful memories from the many exciting things we did way up in the Rockies.

We passed through Denver and were driving into the towering mountains as our Volkswagen engine began having difficulty with acceleration. Dad quickly expressed his concern to us. The high altitude was affecting the flow of air into the carburetor and we were not sure if we were going to make it up the mountain. Everyone was alarmed as we could feel and see that we were driving nearly straight up. I could hear and feel the car shifting down from fourth gear to third. When I heard Dad shift down to second my concern kicked into high gear. What took place next produced the most panic of all. As we drove up another large incline the vehicle was acting more problematic than ever. Then, I heard and felt what I hoped I wouldn't.

Dad shifted down into first gear maximizing the engines power just enough to keep pulling us up the steep Colorado Rocky Mountain. We moved at a frighteningly slow pace of ten miles per hour as close to the right edge of the highway as possible. Dad began praying out loud and we all joined in, silently praying to God with him. Amazingly, we felt our Heavenly Father intervene as our prayers were answered and somehow we made it all the way up. We were thankful and incredibly relieved as we immediately began to gain momentum and remarkably reached our destination.

At the break of day the following morning, Dad took the VW van to a nearby mechanic who checked out the carburetor and adjusted the timing so the van would function in altitudes of 7,000 to 11,000 feet. Happily, there were no more difficulties driving through all of the resorts from Colorado Springs to Estes Park and other interesting places.

The mechanic helped us learn a valuable lesson. When traveling into the high mountain climate and thinner air, it is a necessary safety measure to have the engine's timing adjusted for sake of the proper mixture of air intake.

Oxygen becomes a great deal thinner to humans in mountainous terrain, which I also noticed during the first couple of days, especially during vigorous activity such as hiking longer distances or jogging.

Once we arrived safely, we were now around eighty miles west of Denver, high up into those beautiful hills and temporarily enjoying living in a nice condo at Copper Mountain. We had a wonderful time climbing and I thought of John Denver's popular song, "Rocky Mountain High," throughout our unique vacation trip.

Dad, Brad, Molly, and I took our first hike up a high mountain. It was extraordinary being welcomed by a big blanket of snow in the normally warm month of June. We drove to the top of Pikes Peak where Mom and Dad explained in detail to me the stunning scenery of nature. What an awesome time we treasured.

Another example of God's protection was on a road trip from Indiana to Florida when I was a week away from my sixteenth birthday. My Aunt Nancy and Uncle Marvin were making a permanent move from Indiana and invited me to drive down with them to the Sunshine State to experience the journey and to spend time with my relatives. Before leaving, we shared a prayer for God's protection and his traveling mercies throughout our lengthy trip. As we were more than half way to our destination and getting more excited by the mile, we heard a car frantically honking at us. My aunt and uncle observed that the driver behind us was desperately waving for us to pull the car over. Uncle Marvin quickly pulled off to the side of the road. A piece of cardboard had attached itself to our scorching hot tail pipe. It caught fire and was dangerously close to the gas tank. As my uncle abruptly slowed down, the cardboard fell off and the fire extinguished itself.

    I thank God that it was a visible fire that could be seen from the car behind us and allowed them to alert us of the impending danger. We had a full tank of gas with a piece of burning cardboard attached to the tail pipe. Yet no life-threatening explosion took place. Once again with God's protection we were safe. God is faithful and ever-present. I sometimes wonder how many times the lord has angels here to protect us from danger and physical harm. God is good all the time.

Chapter 12 My CB Radio

When I was 12 years old I really wanted a CB radio for Christmas. Mom and Dad gave me the impression that owning one would not come to fruition. Just as I was about to accept the idea that my dream of owning this hip broadcast communication gadget was off, at least for another year, my father surprised me by stating that my last Christmas present was awaiting my discovery in the bedroom. My extended family--Mom's parents, aunts, uncles and cousins--entered the big bedroom with me. They sure enjoyed watching my exhilaration. Was I really hearing an actual CB Radio? It certainly sounded like the truckers' channel nineteen as it was clearly blasting precisely what I hoped, but didn't expect, to hear. Yes, I *was* hearing a real, live, brand new CB radio. Wow! Was I ever wound up!

Mom and Dad had even put the icing on the cake by purchasing, and secretly installing, a forty foot tower. This enabled me to proudly transmit thirty miles in all directions. A kind man named Bob Eliot put the tower up and we soon became friends. Dad showed me the basics of operating the CB and my Aunt Nancy had me Braille a little directory. It included all of the official two-way communication numbers and their meanings. For example, some one might say, "What's your 1020?" which means, "What is your exact location?"

It was all brand new and extremely exciting. This present was my most electrifying one throughout my childhood. Even with this precious gift, I was taught early in life the birth of Jesus is the real reason for our Christmas season.

Our small hometown had a well-known, respected emergency radio team known as ERT. Their primary purpose was to assist people traveling through our area during inclement weather, which occurred nearly every winter. The members of the group allowed me to become involved.

My gift was perfect timing with the majority of my two-week Christmas and New Year vacation still remaining. ERT had set up their trailer at a truck stop and for a small donation the general public could enjoy hot chocolate, coffee, and donuts. I spent several hours during my extended break helping out our valued club while making many brand new friends. The adults sure did get a kick out of this 12-year-old blind kid who became a CB-a-holic! Reflecting back, I think the CB was another one of those keys that unlocked the passion of radio I had deep inside me.

Chapter 13 Blake's Broadcast Career

It all began less than three months before I turned 15. In two weeks school was letting out for summer vacation. I was thrilled for the pure motivation that summer vacation brings to nearly everyone because of being able to throw away the common academics for nearly three months.

My brand new friend, puberty, had grown my body four inches taller and twenty pounds heavier. I was especially delighted that it had lowered my voice an entire octave, which happened to be the helpful transformation that accelerated my broadcast ambition right on up to the top.

I became fascinated with the idea of being on the airwaves when I was just nine years old. I enjoyed it when a DJ could make me chuckle or when they would play my favorite tune. Radio broadcasters were normally nice to me on the phone when I would call in because they observed my complete curiosity and delight in their profession.

I began keenly expressing my desire to my parents to attend summer school at the J. Everett Light Career Center in Indianapolis. The career center took great pride in teaching high school juniors and seniors the art of broadcasting in their state-of-the-art radio and television facilities. I knew that I could gain considerably through their guidance.

The center was 12 miles from home and just two miles away from the Indiana School for the Blind. Dad told me that if I could convince Mr. Austin, the career center principal, to allow me in two years early him and Mom would drive me to and from all 40 days of summer school. I took Dad's offer seriously so with pleasure I was up for the challenge of selling Mr. Austin on the idea; because broadcasting was my passion that I absolutely wanted to pursue. I told Mr. Austin he could count on me to earn an A+ and that I would do my very best to be an encouragement to the class.

Following my sales pitch to Mr. Austin, I was given the green light to enroll for the summer. My excitement was overwhelming as my radio broadcasting dream was finally becoming a reality after five years of pure hope.

High school radio in Indiana is the best around because of its hefty popularity combined with the competitive tone in the Hoosier state. There are six high schools in central Indiana that have real radio stations. They clearly broadcast a fifteen-mile radius in all directions with the potential of thousands of listeners.

I could not have asked for a better instructor than Mr. John R. King. All of his students used to tell him that his middle initial stood for "Radio." Mr. John Radio King enjoyed being our teacher. It was evident through his teaching style that he was not only interested in his subject area, but he showed great interest in the lives of all of his students.

I was barely 16-years-old and at the mike at WJEL, J Everett Light Radio in 1980. Hosting the four-hour show was the highlight of my tenth grade year.

At the center I was received quite well by the radio and television students. I enjoyed trying to keep the sighted students in my class at ease by making them laugh with my goofy blind humor. My silliest attempt was when they would occasionally show something as a visual example and I would say I was having difficulty seeing their demonstration. That one always got a chuckle.

During my first year in radio, my new high school friend, Kate Rogers, was my main source of encouragement in the radio and television classes. She generously volunteered much of her free time to help me practice. Kate took transmitter readings, completed our program logs, and flawlessly read WJEL's two newscasts each hour. She expressed her interest in learning how to read and write Braille so I spent some time working with her on this constructive mission. I was amazed at how quickly she picked up something many consider to be a foreign language.

What is truly remarkable is that Kate learned to write Braille with a slate and stylus. This is the most difficult Braille tool but it was the only light, portable device available at the time. It weighed under a half pound.

My tenth grade year at the Indiana School for the Blind was filled with excitement. A couple days a week after school, one of our ISB staff members would transport me two miles to the J. Everett Light Career Center so I could host a four-hour radio show. This was my second year on FM 89.3 WJEL. Our station had consistent listeners, including my schoolmates, who occasionally flattered me by treating me with celebrity status.

I proudly made A's in radio and productively earned a few helpful high school credits on a course which eventually played a part in my lengthy broadcasting profession.

WJEL has grown into a powerful signaled radio station that can be heard throughout the Indianapolis area, as well as worldwide through the Internet. Mr. King was recognized and awarded with the honor of being Teacher of the Year in Washington Township Schools in Indianapolis. He taught at the J. Everett Light Career Center for 33 years retiring in 2008. I am pleased to say that we remain good friends today.

Kate has continued to do well in life. She received her college degree from Ball State University and has remained in broadcasting. She currently works for WIPB TV-49 in Muncie, Indiana. Kate has been married for more than twenty years and has a grown daughter out of high school.

One day, at the beginning of public school, Mr. King informed me about a part-time job at the large ice skating rink six miles from home. He encouraged me to apply as he thought I would benefit from having a paid opportunity in which to practice my disc jockey skills.

When I arrived at my interview, accompanied by my brother Brad, a confident six-feet-five-inch tall man named Whitey seemed to have no reservations about my blindness. I convinced him that I would be able to find the right records and tapes and that I could successfully run the equipment. I also assured him that my family was willing to assist in getting me to and from the ice skating rink so he would not have to be concerned about my dependability.

What an exciting September as I had successfully transitioned from the blind school to public school. And now I was working as a paid, live disc jockey! I profitably landed a part time, paying responsibility which would help me to have spending freedom with funds I would take personal pride in earning. Not only did I make a little more than minimum wage, but much to my pleasure, I also earned the right to eat free food from the well-stocked snack bar. To this day my mouth still waters when I think of those delicious jalapeño nachos. What a tasty treat!

After only two weeks of working at the ice skating rink I received an unexpected reward from my boss Whitey--A raise in my pay. He called me into his office and said that he was pleasantly surprised by my performance and attitude. I chuckled and questioned, "You didn't think a blind dude could spin records, Whitey?"

He laughed along with me while firmly shaking my hand. Whitey was a former professional hockey player and was currently coaching a winning high school hockey team in addition to being the head honcho at the skatium.

I learned quite a bit about the ins and outs of hockey and enjoyed hearing about the different teams that played. It was exciting since I had never been given much visual explanation about the game of hockey before working at the 'skadium'. It showed me how new adventures can lead to many new experiences!

The primary ages of my skating audience ranged from ten to eighteen-years-old. The skaters made many requests and dedications to their special skating partners. The best experience of this job I didn't even consider, until years later. I enjoyed making a great number of friends while working as the skating rink's DJ. However, I never realized the positive impression I made on many of our guests. Occasionally, I am informed of such when coming in contact with someone who skated at the ice rink during my two year DJ tenure.

A few years ago I had the pleasure of communicating with a successful businessman named Chris Young. With the sound of gratification in his voice Chris said, "I never introduced myself to you, but I took enjoyment in watching as you would set up our favorite requests and dedications at the Carmel Ice Skadium."

Chris was five years younger and in junior high the first time he first saw me at the ice rink. He said I had served as a source of inspiration to him and his friends by not allowing my sight impairment to stop me from earning a paycheck. Discussions like this one have always served as continued sources of encouragement for me.

Chris and I have become good friends. Not only did I have an opportunity to inspire him, but he has motivated me as well. Chris is an awe-inspiring parent and a high-quality hard worker.

Following high school graduation, I moved to Austin, Texas, just three driving hours away from my immediate family in Dallas. This was much closer than the previously extended sixteen hours of driving from Indiana. My parents heard tremendous reports about Chris Cole Rehabilitation Center for the Blind. This facility provided the best faculty to teach visibly impaired people valuable skills, including independent living, mobility, woodworking, small engine work, etc. I didn't take much advantage of this learning opportunity because I quickly became distracted by a pleasantly unexpected break to perform my passion--commercial radio broadcasting. Yes! A real paycheck for being on the radio. The first month I lived in Austin I was granted the incredible opportunity with KHFI Radio—otherwise known as the number one rated K-98.

Roger Garrett was the program director who hired me. He was not just a person in charge, but was also an individual who had great broadcasting talent and a big booming voice to work with. Roger was on the air from three to seven p.m., known as afternoon drive time. I thought he sounded superb on the airwaves and I observed how he actually practiced what he preached to me during our coaching and development sessions. Roger truly set a supreme example for me to follow.

I was pleased that I had applied with my favorite Austin station as my ambition paid off precisely like I hoped it would. My assignment was to be the on-air personality Monday through Friday from nine to noon and on Saturday nights from seven to midnight.

Not only did I get the luxury of working as a disc jockey with my favorite format of Top 40 hit music, I was also responsible for some commercial production assignments that included providing the voice for local advertisements. The best part was the development I received to sharpen critical skills which allowed me to continue on my journey deeper into the radio industry.

Just shy of my nineteenth birthday, I landed my very first commercial station job at K-98 Radio in Austin, TX. This was the stepping stone in my broadcast career.

One of the greatest memories I have from working at K-98 involved the weekday morning man Dave Jarott. He was a funny, talented guy who quickly became a mentor and friend. I enjoyed learning from him and cannot recall a day that he didn't have me rolling with laughter prior to the start of my airtime. Dave had a true wit for helping me sell blind humor. He felt completely at ease around me and was not too concerned about the political correctness of whether or not to tell a great blind Blake joke. I really believe that his humor helped many of our listeners find a positive perspective on my visual impairment.

Dave taught me how to sell the upside of being blind by poking a little fun, but not so much as to cause overkill on the subject. One selling point of my blindness was that, though my life was different from most of my listeners, I was "Outta Sight" as opposed to having no sight. As long as my humor isn't too over the top silly, I generally make sighted people around me feel comfortable.

With the help of the television press in Austin I was able to challenge sighted and non-sighted people to excel. This is a positive benefit to me being blind. Helping others to shine and also exert maximum effort to overcome obstacles is an enjoyable part of my existence. This has especially become my mission during my adult life. Because I am sightless and I am able to function fairly normally I consider myself extra blessed to be a source of motivation for people from all walks of life. I am delighted that I realize the true challenge and encouragement that I am able to provide to others because it also helps me to perform the best I possibly can. I get excited when I am able to teach my skills to people who are, in their minds, less challenged than me. I only wish I had realized this characteristic as much during my youth.

Celebrating my nineteenth birthday on the radio gave me additional dialogue to share with my listeners the day before the big day. Listeners react in many different ways when it comes to interacting with on-air personalities. Some listeners never call in, some call in often, and some listeners even send things in to their favorite radio hosts.

Kathleen, one of my listeners, decided she wanted to make my birthday extra special so she made a German chocolate cake and dropped it off at the station for me to enjoy. It smelled delicious.

Though it was a kind gesture, I declined to take part in eating the cake as I do not feel completely comfortable eating things people make at home if I have not had the pleasure of meeting them. However, the rest of the radio station staff was not as worried and they all took enjoyment in devouring what turned out to be a harmless, mouth-watering birthday cake.

I'm glad that no one ribbed me about choosing on losing the generous birthday treat I chose to decline.

By age 19 I had already learned a little hard truth concerning blindness. I observed early in life that being totally blind in both eyes was an unfamiliar subject to reflect on with anyone who had not at least known, or even more significantly worked with, a visually impaired person. This reality was my motive for keeping the program director, Billy Thorman, completely in the dark about my sight impairment until we had actually had the opportunity to meet.

Billy and I had a very positive introduction. I firmly shook his hand as if there was nothing especially unique about me. When Billy realized I was blind he dealt with this unexpected surprise quite well. While he was taken aback he honestly didn't show it. I would come to learn that he was a man that followed through on his word, as opposed to giving good lip service and making empty promises. This is what truly made Billy Thorman stand out in a special way.

Doing my best to communicate confidence to Billy, I blurted out, "So, do I begin this week or next?" Yes, this was a bit presumptuous of me but I had no doubt in my mind that I could perform well. Billy's reaction was upbeat and positively inquisitive. He asked me what special needs I had that we could address in order to make the job go smoothly. His questioning inspired me and it also gave me hope that he was not opposed to hiring a blind disc jockey.

A few days later I began working for KTFM, the number one rated San Antonio station with a dominant one hundred thousand watts. It had the most power of any FM signal I had been on prior to this exciting opportunity.

Some of my best memories are from my very first air shift on KTFM. A big part of my thrill was how much my life had drastically changed from just one year earlier when I was living in Indianapolis.

My mission was simple - work hard every day to show Billy Thorman he had made the right decision by giving me a break to shine, despite my challenge of being blind. Billy even went the extra mile by providing me with a show producer whose duties were to set me up each hour for the full 60 minutes of music and commercials. Various college students usually filled this role.

My producer would read our upcoming song titles and the approaching commercial out-cues onto a blank cassette tape for me to listen to. This enabled me to work independently for forty-five minutes as I operated the broadcast equipment by myself. It also freed up my right hand to read or do whatever they wanted or needed to do for most of the hour. My assistant additionally helped me by completing our paperwork with the required program logs. These extraordinary individuals helped me to enjoy my job even more with our entertaining conversation. Through our combined efforts we never missed a beat.

Several months later, while riding in Billy's car, he told me that he liked my positive and slightly over-confident approach in our very first meeting. He had never worked with a blind person before I walked into his office and I was happy when I learned that Mr. "Boss Man" Billy was pleased that I was on his team.

I spent the next four years as a disc jockey for KTFM, formerly part of the Waterman Broadcasting Company. This opportunity provided me with my first full-time employment as a commercial disc jockey. I am eternally grateful to Billy for taking a gamble on me that ultimately made both of us winners.

Today, Billy resides in Fort Worth, Texas, about 40 miles from where I live. We remain close friends to this day.

Conveniently across the hall from KTFM was their sister station KTSA. The powerful KTSA AM-550 was popular as it covered 93 counties in Texas and a portion of Mexico.

For two years I worked seven to midnight as an on-air personality playing requests and dedications. My show on KTSA became popular and attracted a good age group as we played the best variety of tunes from three full decades of music. Because KTSA's signal blanketed so much territory, especially after sunset, it made my job extra exciting to communicate with local people as well as those who were many miles away. The most exciting long distance reach was saying hello to my little brothers, Bryce and Brock, living in Dallas. They would listen to me on their radio until it was time for them to go to sleep at night. My brothers found it quite amazing that even though I lived and worked 260 miles away from them, we could still be connected through the powerhouse station that was strong enough to bring my voice right into their bedroom each evening.

Each week KTSA put together a breakfast and dinner broadcast. I always got a kick out of people saying when they met me at these functions that I didn't sound blind. And of course, we would laugh it off after I enjoyed replying, "How is a blind person supposed to sound?"

My family drove down to visit me in San Antonio for a few days during their Christmas break and stopped by the station during my shift. I was delighted to put Bryce, age 12, on the radio so that he could enjoy the buzz of broadcasting for those many miles on our leading signal. Brock picked out a tune from our huge tape rack for me to dedicate to him.

My parents allowed Bryce to attend our special restaurant of the week, one of our favorites, Grandy's, for the Friday morning breakfast broadcast. At these remote events we would surprise our listeners with special celebrity guests. This particular Friday was a visit from Mean Joe Green. Bryce got to shake his hand and received an autograph. He thought that his big brother Blake was pretty cool.

San Antonio is where I earned my handle, Blazin' Blake. A good friend, DC, who loved radio, began calling me by that name because he noticed I took maximum pleasure in blazing trails in the workplace. I'm grateful to my friend as this name has proven simple to remember with nearly everyone ages five to ninety-five.

As I ended my eight-year radio career working with four radio stations in San Antonio, I wondered what was going to happen in the next chapter of my broadcasting life.

In December of 1991, I officially entered the fifth largest broadcast market in America: Dallas/Fort Worth. Making it even more inviting was my immediate family residing here. Now my voice would only need to travel fifteen short miles instead of the two hundred sixty it had to journey to reach their radio from San Antonio.

Dallas/Fort Worth was the highpoint of my radio profession. It took me several years and attempts to break into this massive market. I launched my DFW broadcast calling with KODZ, Oldies 94.9. Phil Hall was the gracious individual who hired me. He had listened to my radio work that I had recorded onto keepsake cassettes. Those tapes featured my voice on the Austin and San Antonio airwaves.

We broadcasters all know how enjoyable it is to save those memories, but even more important is how incredibly useful these cassettes can be. They provide all of the necessary proof needed to help seal the deal with a fresh broadcast opportunity.

Phil Hall had previously worked with a blind person and was therefore comfortable with my visual impairment. He did not doubt my abilities.

Upon being hired, I was introduced to a radio legend, Mr. Wolfman Jack. Little did I know I was about to have the privilege of not only working with this radio legend, but he was about to become a good friend. This was an absolute highlight in my broadcasting career. I became familiar with Wolfman Jack at the early age of nine and now he was in my presence. How truly amazing this reality was!

Wolfman Jack and I got to be good buddies in 1992 during my first DFW radio gig, at station KODZ-Oldies-94.9. There was never a dull moment working with this legend of broadcasting.

Wolfman's show followed mine every Saturday. His voice sparked the airwaves at seven p.m. He generally arrived at least an hour before his shift to get prepared and to play his usual tricks on me. He acted a bit fascinated at how a visually impaired person could function so well. Wolf had never worked with a blind individual before and he got a big kick out of switching my Braille labels all around the radio consul. I would go along with his trickery and act confused, but fortunately I knew my way around the radio board well enough that he did not cause me to make any embarrassing mistakes.

One afternoon I decided it was high time for a fun turnabout, and I was determined to play a trick on the Wolf. While the long version of the 1972 hit *Nights in White Satin* was playing, I purposefully turned the monitors down really low. I engaged the Wolf into a conversation asking him about his week and he began talking, paying no attention to the fact that a song was playing on the air. It was like two old friends sitting around a kitchen table having a nice conversation without a care in the world. I anxiously waited for the part of the song when the mysterious deep voice would boom out the lyrics "breathe deep." Wolf was sitting across from me on a tall stool. I could hardly wait for the shocker and kept a straight face. During the completely silent part of the song, only a split second before the big booming voice was ready to blast those words, I cranked up the super sounding JBL speakers located just three feet above Wolf's head to their maximum gust. At last, those words "breathe deep" bellowed like a freight train driving right through the studio from the state-of-the-art air monitor. Just as I had hoped, Wolf jumped right out of his seat completely in a state of shock. I learned some choice words that night.

"Wolf, you don't mind if I get you back every once in awhile now do you?" I asked with a contented chuckle. I am thankful he did not have a heart attack. We laughed and we laughed until my stomach felt as if I had worked out a vigorous one hundred crunches. This was typical of every Saturday, having a blast and laughing until our bellies could not take it any longer.

Outside of the radio studio I spent some quality time with Wolf. My most enjoyable memory was fishing together on Lake Grapevine. We did not catch too many fish but we truly had a pleasurable time. I wish I had recorded all of the stories Wolf shared with me about his exhilarating radio career as it was a true treasure trove. I think of Wolf often. Of course I wish he were still with us but what great memories I will always enjoy. I know for certain we touched each other's lives in a very positive way.

My next radio job was at 106.1 KISS-FM in Dallas. On air was a blast at KISS-FM. I enjoyed talking with people on the phones, playing their dedications, and giving them prizes (many of which I couldn't have even afforded to purchase myself).

Molly, who was my right hand person when we were kids, was also my radio show producer during my first year at KISS-FM. It was really cool being able to once again count on her to be my required assistant just like when we were children. She always went the extra mile to help me succeed with school fund raising projects and continued

Blake and Molly

doing so at KISS-FM. We enjoyed getting to know each other again as adults. I appreciated and benefited from her extraordinary organizational skills. This useful strong point she encompassed was in an area I considered to be my weakness and we worked well together. Many of the best complements my superiors honored me with through the seven years I was employed at KISS-FM were given to me when

Molly and I were a team. She received a well-deserved employment opportunity and moved away from the Dallas area.

I got a big kick out of working with Kidd Kraddick in the morning. I enjoyed him for three exceptional reasons: His great sense of humor, his approachability, and how he treated me as anyone else. When Kidd would sit by me at a station luncheon, he would occasionally sneak my fork into something that wasn't on my plate to surprise me. He enjoyed watching my facial expressions as I entered the unknown food zone. Luckily, I am not picky and enjoyed those witty pranks. He was never apprehensive about potentially offending me just because I am blind. Even though he has been in the spotlight for a long time he did not have an inflated ego and I really admire him for that.

Kidd has been on the air in the DFW area for nearly 30 years and has accomplished so very much. He has an organization called *Kidd's Kids*, benefiting terminally ill children. Through his efforts, the organization is successful in raising several thousand dollars each year. This allows these kids to enjoy life for a few days at Disney World in Orlando Florida while building eternal memories with their families. These outings are paid for by listener's donations from several special fundraising events throughout the year. I hear the happiness in the voices of those people who gladly support Kidd's passion, realizing the fun the children and their families enjoy.

Members of Kidd's radio team transform into a care team as they accompany and assist parents with their children. This is true caring team effort all of the way.

I have been to Disney World twice - once with family, and again, with a good friend. It is every bit as enjoyable for a person who is blind as it probably is for any individual.

For five years in a row I had the pleasure of filling Kidd's boots for two weeks during his Christmas vacations. Throughout these two weeks it was no trouble at all to work the required 40 hours with my full time job at the bank in addition to helping out at the station. I was usually pretty energetic and now I had accelerated adrenalin from performing my broadcast passion. It was certainly worth being a little tired to communicate with Kidd Kraddick's loyal listeners, many of whom were compassionate, caring people like him. He attracts a positive audience as much as any personality I have ever known.

Kidd is successfully syndicated in many cities besides Dallas/Fort Worth for several years now.

As radio personalities, we are often asked the million-dollar question, "What do you look like?" At least one day out of the year, my listeners had an opportunity to find out. Each Labor Day, I was a part of the local DFW televised portion of our Muscular Dystrophy Telethon. I enjoyed using my Braillewriter on TV while taking donations as they were called in to me. I would then read the names of MDA's givers live on the air, uniquely using my fingers to translate. This distinctive approach sure seemed to encourage lots of people to call in as they observed my true passion for helping MDA. In addition to my work with the telethon, I would also make a financial contribution each year to let people witness me cheerfully putting my money where my mouth was with my on-air dialogue. I am serious with my role in being a Muscular Dystrophy team player and doing as much as I am able to zap this hostile disease.

Chapter 14 Baseball Blake for the Afternoon

I feel close to my Florida family even though we are more than a thousand miles apart. Jennifer and I love to take an annual vacation to Central Florida to enjoy a good visit with all of them.

Our family in Florida includes Aunt Nancy; her husband, Uncle Marvin; cousins Joy and Paul, who have been married for more than thirty years; and their sons, Peter and Rhett. Peter is married to Gretchen and they have been blessed with a dear daughter named Bella.

One special occasion during my Florida vacation, I had the pleasurable opportunity to bond with my then fourteen-year-old cousin Rhett. Throughout my retreat, I particularly enjoyed hearing Rhett discuss his career aspiration to become a chiropractor. Even though I was delighted with his career goal, I enjoyed kidding with him about all the fun he would miss out on by not choosing a splendid line of work like being a radio DJ. Rhett's mother, Joy, knew that there was a lot more security in his professional preference than mine, so she kindly asked me to cease my verbal nonsense. I knew she was right on so I stopped the teasing. Even though our career choices had no commonality, I really got a kick out of discovering our coincidence: Just like my fourteen-year-old cousin, my career goal set reached its highest peak and became finalized when I was the same age. My hope began when I was nine; however, my adolescent voice was clearly far from catching up to my vision for another five years.

This precise Florida visit also contains another amusing memory for me. My occasion to bond with Rhett happened to be right in the middle of his middle school baseball season. Joy was responsible for finding volunteers to perform a variety of duties at the games and she asked me if I would please be the booth announcer for a live game. Rhett echoed his mom expressing the same request. He figured it would be a piece of cake for me to wolf on the mic at the game since I had been a radio DJ now for nearly eighteen years. Fresh challenges are exciting for me and this assignment absolutely fit the bill for two reasons: I know very little about baseball and I am blind.

Now, it is not as dumb an idea as you would think. Uncle Marvin ran the scoreboard beside me and he has a vast knowledge on the subject of baseball and the jargon to go along with the sport. With this winning combination and team effort, he could communicate to me what I needed to convey to the crowd. Uncle Marvin and I embraced our brand new challenge and willingly accepted our mission.

As luck would have it, Mom and I were together on this trip. She sat in the booth with us, along with her two sisters, which really made this event an extra special occasion for all of us.

With Marvin's excellent help, I confidently announced all of the player's names with enthusiasm. We got into a rapid rhythm with Marvin passing on to me what to say after each play. His voice didn't come through the speakers because of my quick finger operating the microphone's on and off switch. I had a blast being the convincing announcer known as Baseball Blake for the duration of the game. Through Uncle Marvin's eyes, along with his assortment of baseball lingo and great sense of humor, I was able to comfortably and believably boom out all kinds of brand new baseball terminology on this lively afternoon. No spectator had a clue that there was a blind dude in the booth behind that mic. But the most comical component to me was that my limited knowledge on baseball didn't deter my delivery at all.

I believe that my pleasure from this live occasion probably resembles the buzz actors and actresses encounter when they perform as an authority on a theme that they, in many instances, aren't especially knowledgeable on.

How do you face challenges that come your way?

First, be determined to meet the challenge. You can do it! Remember, as Joe Sabah says, "You don't have to be great to start, but you have to start to be great!" Second, you need to have a team environment. Decide who can you collaborate with and who will help you to see your challenge more clearly. I would not have been successful without my caring Uncle Marvin by my side as my necessary Seeing Eye person. Third, when faced with a challenge – dive in! I love the saying, "Anything worth doing is worth doing poorly until you can learn to do it well." Do it and grow in the process. Finally, think about what worked well and how you felt about it. As you reflect on successful events, you can begin to anchor those positive feelings and draw upon them when faced with future challenges. I don't know that I will ever call another baseball game, but I am up for the challenge!

Are you up for the challenges facing you? Rhett certainly was. He is now a licensed chiropractor and massage therapist just as he had hoped and planned for in the eighth grade.

Chapter 15 The Real World of Business

I soon discovered that life as a disc jockey was really exciting; however, it had a major drawback. Tenures of being on the radio did not usually last for more than two years at one place. I desired stability. I wanted to work full-time with a stable job while working part time on the radio if possible.

Fortunately, Bank of America came to my rescue. Recruiters from the bank were among those listening to me speaking at a local job-finding convention where I had stated my desire to work in customer service. A couple of weeks later my day excelled from good to great when I received the exciting phone call I had been hoping for. I then completed several initial interviews and passed the bank's required written assessment tests.

No other blind people were employed in the call center of the bank; however, I convinced them to open up a career door for me. The bank and its employees assisted me by providing all of the necessary adaptive technology. We worked well together. I had superior trainers who were patient and I gave them 100% of my efforts.

Prior to working at the call center, I had always thought of myself as a wonderful listener. Working at the call center provided me

Adaptive technology is a wonderful thing. Where would we be without the contributions of others?

with a wake-up call that my listening was not as great as I thought it was. This job demanded personal mastery of the art on how to listen intently. In only three months, while working in customer service at the bank, I learned how to keenly pay attention to what people were really saying. I also learned how to maintain better focus on our conversation and to consider the inconvenience that someone other than me was experiencing. I was happy when I could resolve a customer-related problem and could often hear their relief come right through the telephone. Our call center employed 500 people and I managed to maintain my productivity in the top 15 percent status for five years in a row. My employers acknowledged my hard work with several awards and financial bonuses throughout our relationship.

Another element of extra encouragement I valued was earning the responsibility to train several of Bank of America's associates. This was when I discovered my effectiveness in coaching sighted people. My unique situation of being totally blind actually accelerated the learning curve. The associates I coached had not worked with a sightless person before and they were all quite attentive. Of course I wanted to put them at ease, as well as boost their confidence, so I would tell them, "If blind Blake can do this job, I believe that you can too. Don't you agree?" I would almost always observe their approval through a stress-free chuckle.

I wish everyone had the opportunity to work in customer service for at least a year. It was a personal relationship enhancer for me. My ten-year tenure with the customer service profession transformed me into an improved compromiser who was then able to expand on our client's personal relationships.

In October 1999, I was presented with the Mayor's Award for excellent work ethics and for overcoming out-of-the-ordinary challenges. The primary key for winning this prestigious award was my rigorous work schedule. I was currently employed full-time with Bank of America in customer service, while also juggling my pleasurable part-time radio career on the number one rated radio station in the Dallas Fort worth market, KHKS' KISS-FM.

I got a kick out of telling people that I had a good full-time job so that I could support my radio broadcasting addiction. I was grateful for the extra income as well. It allowed me to pursue my passion for radio. My two combined occupations helped me be the victor of this constructive reward. What an encouraging surprise this was for me.

I recall the awesome food at the banquet along with an expanded occasion I was granted; A chance to encourage a nice crowd of more than three hundred people with my speech of pure gratitude. I spoke about positive team effort and how truly effective it has been in my life. Here was yet another God-given opportunity for me to inspire others to work to their full potential on behalf of those with and without physical challenges.

Chapter 16 Bringing Your "A" Game to Life's Challenges

Convincing employers to take a good look at how much blind people can accomplish is still an obstacle, but so much less so with the aid of our remarkable technology today. Each time I get a new job, I encounter the same apprehension sighted people have concerning working with someone sightless. Unfortunately, many sighted people do not give the blind adequate opportunities in the workplace. Due primarily to the rational reason that most people haven't ever had a circumstance to gain knowledge on today's helpful technology and how much we are able to additionally achieve with it.

Once I am given the chance to prove to an employer my abilities, along with the required modifications when necessary, their apprehension completely vanishes. The people who have given me opportunities have earned my respect and admiration because they have added value to my life. This teamwork also encourages my colleagues when they observe successful accomplishment and productivity. I am confident that I attach value to any company and serve its customers well. It is fulfilling to know that through my positive attitude and best efforts in the workplace God has enabled many others to see the light through my loss of sight.

I was able to help blaze the trail for Stephen Kerr, a totally blind friend, into commercial radio. He works at Entercom's radio KKMJ-MAGIC-95.5 in Austin, Texas. In the summer of 1983, I was nearly nineteen years old working with K-98 and received positive press on a televised news segment. This reduced thousands of people's apprehension by helping them to understand that radio was an excellent and feasible career for blind communicators.

Stephen has a great attitude and works very hard. He works for caring people who have helped him excel in the broadcasting business. One outstanding person who helped Stephen tremendously is a gentleman by the name of Darrell Heckendorf, an engineer determined to take on the challenge of modernizing a blind-friendly radio control room for my buddy.

A few years ago I had the pleasure of meeting with Stephen and Darrell to sample Darrell's creation for myself. His solution to our challenge was simplistic and completely obliging to me as well. Darrell had laid a full-sized piece of Plexiglas over the computer touch screen and cut finger-sized holes precisely where the functionality is located. A blind person can easily familiarize themselves with the screen by memorizing the exact count to the correct hole in the Plexiglas to execute the specific task required. Yeah!! No more Braille labels that easily fall off! For further convenience, this template folds up and out of the way for those who don't call for this modification. It is a cheap and simple solution to assist those visually challenged in radio broadcasting. It even eliminates the need for an assistant, which I had to employ throughout my 22-year radio career. I look forward to using this adaptation some day in my own radio setup.

  I often sit and think about the people like Darrel who make such great contributions for the advancement of others. What would life be like without those caring people who focus their inventions on helping others who face unique physical challenges? I thank God for these extraordinary people and an extra special blessing I wish upon Darrell Heckendorf.

Chapter 17 New York City

The first of June in 1996 was an extra special day for my family. My brother Bryce graduated from the United States Military Academy (USMA) at West Point in New York, 60 miles outside of New York City. It was a crisp, sunny, 75 degree day as we celebrated among the breathtaking Catskill Mountains.

Many of our relatives, including Mom's 90-year-old dad who we grandkids called Pap, joined us for this extraordinary event. We were proud of Bryce for his hard work and achievement and thrilled to celebrate his accomplishment.

Immediately following the ceremony, Bryce invited his brothers, sister, and sister-in-law to join him in driving one hour to New York City. This was an extremely exciting evening for me. I had been in radio broadcasting at this point for fifteen years. My friends who were in the radio profession and I often talked about the cutting edge sound of the number one broadcast market and largest city in our nation, New York City. I had often enjoyed hearing many of the talented radio legends on New York's three big AM blow torch signals. And also listening to pre-recorded shows broadcasted from New York; however, I had never had the opportunity to enjoy the buzz of actually being right there. Now, here I was, listening intently to live local New York City radio on my own Sony headset. The air talent was impressive even during the overnight hours when talent is usually defined by the demeaning word ROOKIE.

I am glad I got to enjoy this thrill to hear the finest in broadcasting when I did. This unique opportunity occurred only months before what many of us broadcasters consider the demise of live local radio.

Bryce escorted us to the lobby of the World Trade Center but the elevator was turned off for the evening. It didn't stop us from having a blast as we boarded the subway which became another highlight for me. Only two minutes after we began moving, a man stood up in the train chanting, "I'm a homeless in the street with nothing to eat. All I'm looking for is a tasty treat." I don't remember the rest of his rap but it sure brought a big grin to my face. It made the subway experience for me as big as New York City itself.

At nearly two o'clock in the morning we retreated to a huge downtown McDonald's restaurant to order what turned out to be one of the best hot and delicious chicken sandwiches I had ever eaten. This was partly because I was starved and positively due to the pure excitement of eating in the heart of New York City after midnight. Frank Sinatra was right on when he sang about the city that never sleeps. Our exclusive nighttime adventure made a fond lifetime memory for all of us.

Bryce now has a wonderful wife of over sixteen years, plus three daughters and one son. I sure love and enjoy the full six-pack.

Chapter 18 Jennifer

Our Heavenly Father answers many prayers. I used to pray to find a kind, loving wife and in return I promised to be a faithful, loving husband. My parents also prayed for this void to be filled in my life. In July 2000, while living in Dallas and employed with Bank of America and KISS-FM, our prayers were once again answered.

A letter addressed to me was placed in my KISS-FM mailbox prior to my Saturday and Sunday weekend shifts. Jennifer Gable, a longtime fan of my radio show, was the writer. She did not know her favorite disc jockey was totally blind.

Since I could not read her letter, I asked my assistant to do the honors. Though I could not see my partner's face I could tell by the excitement in Heather's voice, as she read to me, this letter was a keeper. I soon found out that Jennifer was a keeper as well!

In the letter, Jennifer told me about herself including her occupation, high school, and the reasons she enjoyed tuning in to my radio show. She was a six-year listener. I was excited that she exerted extra effort composing such a nice letter for me. Her letter changed our lives and will be kept close to my heart for the rest of my life.

Full of intrigue and excitement, I quickly dictated a response. We soon began talking on the phone and I informed her I was completely blind. Jennifer is sighted, which encouraged me all the more as my condition did not bother her. She took the news just fine and knew that I was not teasing her. This would have been a silly subject for me to fabricate since she would soon find out for herself.

Within a few weeks of chatting we decided to meet in person. My friend Jason drove me to meet her. Her open-mindedness made me want to roll out the red carpet for her. My goal for that evening was to provide a fun first impression that would leave Jennifer a fond memory to treasure for the rest of her life.

We had dinner at Chili's restaurant for our first date. Jason was very enthusiastic about driving us. While he was excited about meeting Jennifer and I together, he received an extra boost of motivation from the free meal he received for serving as the evening's chauffeur. I'm eternally grateful to Jason for his help, which in due course turned out to be even more meaningful than I imagined it would be.

Our ride to the restaurant was exciting as we became acquainted with one another. Jennifer quickly noticed I was "handicapable," thank goodness, and not handicapped. She showed an interest in seeing me again and we soon began dating regularly on Saturday nights. It was important to me that Jennifer initiate things due to our 13 year age difference. To my relief, she informed me that this did not bother her. On Sundays we began attending church together. We could both feel our friendship strengthening. Our conversations became more frequent and deeper. She was very considerate which was easy to observe and appreciate.

Jennifer and I quickly realized that we shared many of the same ideals and hobbies. We discovered we both enjoyed similar music. Her tastes were amazingly broad. Since first meeting, she has exposed me to many classic movie tunes and oldies I had never heard before—even gospel artists who I now thoroughly enjoy listening to.

I had never proposed marriage before and was a bit unsure of the proper procedures. So I called my longtime friend, Johnny Shannon, and asked him about the number of knees required to kneel during a proposal. After a chuckle, he told me one knee was all I would need. I wanted to make sure I did it properly.

It was New Year's Eve 2001 and I had great hopes for how 2002 was going to begin. Jennifer and I went to dinner at Antonio's restaurant with some true friends whom I had let in on the secret earlier that day. I was extremely eager for midnight to arrive. After what seemed like an eternity the clock finally struck the magic hour. I bent down on one knee and asked Jennifer the anticipated question I had been carrying around with me all day. There was complete assurance in her unhesitant, "Yes!"

I learned later that she was beginning to wonder whether I would ever ask her or not, and I'm completely delighted I did.

Jennifer and I were married at First Baptist Church of Carrollton on March 29, 2003. Several years of marriage have gone by and I thank God for her every day. I am also thankful for my radio career, which was instrumental in partnering me with my soul mate. Our music library grows a little larger every year and we really enjoy the hobby of bringing it together from CDs that we own. It includes several of the "Best of the Best" collections. We also enjoy making Christmas compilation CD's and giving them out with Christmas cards to our family and friends. Of course we have some money wrapped up in this leisurely pursuit but we sure enjoy it.

With Jennifer in my life I receive more pleasure than ever. She shares with me what she sees in our world every day, which enables me to realize that the life we have and the world we live in are simply amazing.

Jennifer knows how to give me excellent visual insight with just a few words. She not only has a wonderful knack for describing scenery, but also enjoys helping me maximize my pleasure from the movies we see together.

Many times during a film there is often silence and visual dialogue is taking place. Jennifer quickly fills in those blanks with a two-second nutshell whisper, never distracting anyone near us.

This is a photo memory of the happiest day of my life- marrying my beautiful wife, Jennifer, on March 29, 2003.

While we are driving Jennifer reads the signs and billboards to me. She colorfully explains our surroundings and what businesses there are in unfamiliar areas. She describes what the sky looks like when it is especially beautiful or unique with a storm approaching.

We took memorable pleasure in celebrating our fifth anniversary by enjoying our very first Carnival cruise vacation to Cozumel and Progresso, Mexico.

Wow! Did I ever enjoy a clear visual perspective of those magnificent sights we were surrounded by; all because of her alert and caring explanations. I saw everything I wanted to with Jennifer by my side.

Blake and Jennifer aboard the cruise ship.

Another example of her terrific insight is her interpretation of an Oreo commercial that was playing on TV the other day. It is very common for today's TV commercials to be silent or have few words. This particular advertisement depicted two cops, one African American and one Caucasian, competing to lick the filling out of their Oreo cookies. Without even asking her, Jennifer explained the commercial to me in five seconds flat. This brought a smile to my face as I imagined all the little details of the commercial in my mind—two grown men rushing to devour tiny little goodies, crumbs dropping to the floor, and faces covered in chocolate mush. Quite hilarious!

Chapter 19 Transformation

People often ask me, "Why are you no longer a DJ on the air somewhere?" I'm happy to explain with a story that has an unenthusiastic beginning, but a very positive reassuring ending like some of my favorite trials. If you are experiencing a career transition, or know someone who is, I hope this life lesson that I learned will help.

I, like many others in the industry, keep asking, "Why in the world has broadcasting taken such a turn over the last decade or so?" I've read and heard about the many occupations ranging from the auto industry, to banking, to the broadcasting business, to our medical trade and more. I feel the downbeat blow from consolidations and budget cuts, which lead to layoffs. I believe that technology has certainly helped us more than hurt us, but the steadily improving automation with some of these new machines has definitely taken several jobs away from people. I became personally impacted by these ongoing changes in the summer of 2001.

I had worked with KISS-FM in Dallas Fort Worth for more than seven years, which seemed to me like a respectable milestone that I was excited about continuing. I loved performing each weekend, especially when I had the opportunity to fill the shoes of our morning man, Kidd Kraddick, during his vacations. Then, one day, all three of us part time staff were laid off. This was yet another test along the way to transformation. Transformed people must be resilient and spring back when faced with obstacles and career setbacks.

Over the last several years consolidation and computerized voice tracking has maximized the use of on-air personalities by canning one voice and automating its use on multiple radio stations within the same chain of ownership. One DJ or newscaster can be a talent on two or three radio stations a day, thousands of miles apart. Periodically a listener, who is unfamiliar to this concept, will call the local station hoping to speak with the personality that they are hearing on the air. But that individual is not live or local to chat. Honestly, engaging in on-the-air conversations was one of the many things I enjoyed about being a DJ. I know that radio is only one of many careers being affected in this way.

Much to my surprise, I became reenergized in 2005 concerning my broadcasting career. My radio mentor, John King, asked me to cut a few promos for WJEL. The station was preparing to celebrate their thirtieth anniversary on September 3rd. I was pleased he wanted my participation in their celebration and readily agreed to produce a few promos. I certainly didn't consider that this promo opportunity would be priceless experience in a brand new role known in the broadcasting business as *voice talent imaging*. Imaging is the common word which simply means branding. For example, my voice is instrumental in communicating the purpose of listening to that specific station. In some instances, I might promote the station's upcoming events, contests, or perhaps the stations identifications. Learning this fresh skill and getting some practice was more valuable to me than money would have been at that time. I was also thrilled to be finally concluding my four-year absence from my broadcast profession, or for me a type of hobby. When you truly enjoy what you are doing it seems to go beyond work, resulting in a keen sense of contribution and fulfillment.

Blake and John King

I was hopeful for a new broadcasting channel to fill my vacancy and voice talent imaging was absolutely my answer.

I get a real kick as I reflect upon this coincidence that launched my brand new broadcast niche. Here, more than 20 years after I was an on-air student, my first station to broadcast on was also responsible for being my initial voice imaging assignment. It brought me additional excitement as WJEL received two noticeable power increases since I had been an on-air student. The station benefited from the improved signal.

When I agreed to perform imaging for my long time friend John King at WJEL, I asked my friend Jim, who has a simple production studio in his home, if I could make special use of his facility. He gave me the green light and we had a blast. Since Jim was thirty miles from my residence and I needed additional time in the

Blake performing audio production.

studio, I learned exactly what equipment I required and purchased the right production tools. Now I have my own in-home studio to perform audio production. With expanded use of email, I send my work over to my client in a matter of minutes as opposed to a day or more through the regular mail system. A lesson, which was reinforced to me here, is that there is really no self-made successful person. It takes other people to be a success in life. Think about that. You need colleagues, partners, employees or clients, and possibly all of the above. Collaboration and building strong partnerships such as this are critical to be successful in today's fast paced world of rapid change.

As my friend Zig Ziglar would say, "Learn to win here before going there," and this is precisely what occurred for me. Before long, my next door was opening. Another buddy, Larry, purchased a radio station in Paris, Texas. I sent him a sample to hear from my fresh voice talent branding for WJEL. After listening to it, Larry was confident my imaging would also help him launch his brand new station in a full-size way. I created custom made production for Larry's specific needs and he was pleased with the outcome. These two radio stations were enough to provide plenty of experience and momentum to develop my new knack in broadcasting. John King, plus Larry and Jim, all were active in helping me develop right into voice talent production; yet another career which has transformed into a hobby. My brand new business is called Blazin' Blake Productions, using the radio handle which I am known for on Hit Music stations. My voice is also heard on several commercials broadcast nationwide.

Blazin' Blake Productions is growing and I am pleased to be making progress with this brand new trade. I currently perform voice production for four radio stations and a local TV program. I additionally help people with professional audio on their websites, explaining in ten to sixty seconds a quantity of key benefits that their trade accomplishes. This also keeps my broadcast communication skills sharpened.

That is another life lesson learned: Try to make every engagement or opportunity a win-win. John's request for promos to billboard WJEL's upcoming reunion was the precise push I needed to see my brand new vision through. The personal voice production illustration I am sharing can happen to all of us in a variety of ways. This has really helped me maintain my commitment to staying open-minded. I continue to strive toward personal mastery, good technique, and effective execution in the hopes that what I am able to do is a service to others. It is intriguing how sometimes the occasional unsolicited career changes that we encounter usually find some way to challenge us by making us even stronger, rather than stopping us. I encourage anyone in a job or career transition to be resilient and to positively look for a new door to open when one seems to close. Life is a series of entering and exiting. I have learned how you exit one event or era affects how you enter the next. So exit gracefully and well as you enter into the next opportunity. I have also learned that when we are forced to seek new and perhaps better opportunities, our hidden talents frequently emerge. That is the process of being transformed by turning the lemons of life into lemonade.

Doing our very best to remain hopeful, resilient, confident, and keeping a positive attitude is most important through career changes and professional transformations. I absolutely believe, deep in my spirit, that when one door closes another one is about to open. Very often it will lead to a better situation than you previously had. That open door might be one step away or just around the corner. The main thing is to just hang in there and keep knocking and seeking because a new opportunity IS coming. When it arrives, bury any fear or hesitation you may have regarding change. Embrace it with enthusiasm and meet any learning challenges head on. You'll become transformed in the process…and that's a mighty good thing! As the Bible says, be transformed by the renewing of the mind.

Chapter 20 Leap of Faith

Being a person who's been totally blind since infancy, the unique condition gives me additional opportunities to challenge and inspire people of all ages to set significant goals and to follow through with their action plan. Each September I have the privilege of speaking with a bright group of high school seniors who are together for Camp Enterprise. This three day business education development is sponsored by Rotary Club of Dallas.

In 2010 I was finishing my talk with a segment I call, "Ask the Blind Guy." This is my audience's opportunity to ask me any questions they are curious about regarding what it is like to be totally blind. I always enjoy these questions, especially from junior high and high school students. During this occasion, I was asked something which I had never been asked before; "Blake, is there anything you haven't done on your list of adventures that you want to accomplish"?

Without thoroughly thinking the inquiry through I blurted out the first response that came to mind, "Skydiving." I stated that this would be an adventure with which I've been fascinated for many years. Other than the brief discussion we had regarding this exciting speaking event during our ride home, I didn't even think about my skydiving reply.

Two weeks later, I received a surprise call from Charles with the Rotary Club of Dallas, stating, "We are sponsoring you on a skydive, so when can you go?"

My first thought was, "Wow! Did I really say I wanted to skydive?" I immediately realized yes I did, and now it is time for me to follow through with my spontaneous response to the students. I graciously said thank you very much for this adventure-filled opportunity. We established the best time for my skydive to take place, when I could be accompanied by a willing and qualified instructor. I was happy that my friends, Heather and Michael, from Rotary Club of Dallas wanted to be there for my first skydive experience. Heather had told me all about her first skydive, and she wanted to do it again.

Surprisingly, I became more excited and less nervous each day. I called some friends and family to state that I expected complete safety. But if something should happen, I wanted them to know how very much I cared about our relationship. I knew that if I did have an accident that I was ready to leave this phase of life and be taken to my permanent home. I subsequently paid our bills in advance and even showed my wife, Jennifer, how to pay them online using our computer. Additionally, I showed her how to utilize our phone to pay a few of the bills that can be done through telephone automation. Being blind has helped make it easy for me to take advantage and learn to use technology in useful ways.

As I thought about this, somewhat fearful, goal of skydiving I began envisioning how it could help me to inspire people to dive into their goals and face their fears in life. I asked my good friends, Glen Martin and JD Ryan, if they would make a video recording of this extraordinary event. They quickly agreed and came along on the adventure.

I was grateful to be able to go in one day before my jump. I was driven by my Rotary friend Michael Morelli. It is imperative to have some brief training on how to position my body and what I should generally expect. This was valuable education from my instructor, Ernie Long.

I made some friends that day, people who frequently skydived. I enjoyed their kindness and eagerness to share their experiences with me. They could hardly wait to see me encounter what they knew would be a blast for a blind guy, or anyone for that matter.

The day of the special occasion Glen and I drove out to a peaceful and beautiful wooded area where he often walked. We recorded my feelings before this event took place. It was a beautiful Saturday morning without a cloud in the sky. The winds were gently blowing at eight miles per hour. Glen's awesome interview also captured, in audio, the wonderful sounds of nature--including a distant noise of our public light-rail-transportation-train passing by. After our extraordinary start to an exciting day we got into Glen's car and proceeded to find Skydive Dallas.

I'll never forget how much I enjoyed our one hour drive and visit up to Whitewright, TX. Glen and I talked about the meaning of our life that beautiful morning. We arrived ahead of schedule and enjoyed a quick bite for lunch. Glen and I then walked outside to observe all of the other people skydiving. Our outside temperature was a warm 88 degrees, which felt just right with the light breeze.

JD soon arrived and we all caught up on life because it had been a long time since Glen had seen, or I had heard, JD face to face. *The Dallas Morning News* had graciously agreed to write my story and they were next to appear. I had a detailed interview from a pleasant lady with a cool and memorable name, Holly Hacker.

It was finally time to climb into the plane which seated 23 of us tightly fitted. I was excited to, at last, be taking that leap of faith I had thought about a lot over the past two weeks in anticipation of the unknown. I was fully alert and attentive as we climbed up to 13,500 feet and prepared to jump with my instructor, Ernie.

Our leap into the air was like no other feeling I have ever felt before. For one, the temperature is thirty degrees cooler at 13,500 feet than on the ground. What had been a balmy 88 degrees was now an exhilarating 58.

We hit the air at around 140 miles per hour and maintained that momentum as we dropped for sixty seconds. My hearing was temporarily lost due to the quickly changing pressure. When our parachute deployed I had an opportunity to do all of the old tricks to retrieve my hearing as if I were in a plane descending for landing. My instructor, Ernie Long, began performing exhilarating maneuvers, showing me how much control he had in steering us with the sturdy steering strings attached to our parachute. I got a kick out of quickly turning to the left, then right, followed by moving backwards and forwards. "Wow!" I exclaimed. When we comfortably and safely landed, all of my friends and spectators applauded.

Blake and his skydiving instructor.

I can certainly state that this exceptional experience is among my most exciting, and most valuable, in my lifetime to date. Each time I reflect upon the experience it seems I learn another lesson in how to live my life more fully and to inspire others to enjoy the same. I'm more determined than ever to motivate people to be the best they can be in finding joy in life, at work, at home, and in the community each and every day.

Glen used his remarkable talent, took all of the amazing pictures which he and JD had taken, and produced perfect ten and five minute videos showing and telling my unique story. This keepsake production will always encourage people to dive into their goals and face those fears and challenges which inevitably come our way in life. Without a doubt, when we dive into our goals and face our challenges, it can resemble my skydive experience by becoming "Faith and fun all in one!"

Chapter 21 — The Power of Prayer

God answered my prayer by sending me Jennifer. God is constant and even in the rough times in life He is present. Jennifer and I know that He is beside us at all times and we realize that the power of prayer is often evident in our lives. But one recent instance in particular boldly stands out.

Jennifer and I were discussing some forecasted financial changes which could affect our budget if we weren't careful. The local news reported that electricity bills in North Texas would be jumping 20 percent within the year. We were not looking forward to this increase, as it would directly impact our finances. To make matters even more challenging, two weeks later we received a notice that our rent was to increase by $60 a month, $40 more than we had anticipated from past experiences. This made Jennifer and me way more budget-conscious than usual, but we decided to keep our dinner date and proceeded to our favorite Chinese restaurant.

We always pray before eating, thanking our Heavenly Father for what he has blessed us with today, and praying about life's situations where we know He can make a caring difference. I prayed that we would be able to successfully negotiate with our management the predictable $20 a month increase that we were prepared for.

After supper, our server brought us the bill along with two fortune cookies. Jennifer and I had never taken our fortunes seriously before, even though they usually carried an element of common sense. I was getting ready to do my usual chuckle as Jennifer began to read the fortune to me. Much to my surprise, the fortune was even sweeter than the cookie itself. The tiny piece of paper had the following words in print: *God will help you overcome any hardship.*

I had never received a fortune in a cookie that had a mentioning of God. Nevertheless, what an ideal time for the assurance and a thoughtful reminder that God would help us navigate through our financial hardship.

The next day, I got started on the phone in the hopes that I would be able to talk with someone regarding our rent increase. On my third attempt I communicated with a kind manager who had known about my eight-year tenure and perfect payment status. She promised to review our records and said she would get back with us within a few days. First thing on Monday morning we received a great news phone call. Our apartment-leasing manager informed us that our rent would be increasing only $5 a month. We could not believe our ears…not sixty which had been stated in our note, or even twenty which we would have been okay with…but a barely noticeable $5 increase a month! These additional funds would sure help us tremendously with the pending increase in our electricity bill.

We understood that God would respond to our prayers in some positive way and he certainly did once again. The cost of energy inflated as much as predicted. But with our Lords help Jennifer and I made it through like you will too.

Our God truly helps his followers through hardships. And what became of that piece of paper with our amazing fortune printed on it? It is now taped to our computer screen and serves as a continuous encouraging reminder that we take very seriously.

Here is another true story full of inspiration on the subject of God's intervention. Prior to my birth, Aunt Nancy had considered teaching sightless children at the Indiana School for the Blind. She even took the initiative to visit Michigan State University to gain an accurate understanding of what to expect. This particular school had a special program that produced some of the nation's top-rated teachers for those without sight.

When I became blind, Aunt Nancy realized that my lack of sight and her previous inquiry regarding the teaching of blind students were revelations from God. She believed this was pure confirmation verifying that she should move forward with earning her additional credentials on top of her already existing teaching license. In addition to Aunt Nancy's lengthy teaching career in public schools, she then taught six years at the Indiana School for the Blind.

When I was in junior high and Aunt Nancy was teaching third grade at the blind school, she depended on me to proofread her Braille on her prepared lessons. My fingertips seldom found any mistake because her Braille writing was excellent. After I was finished with my proofreading, Aunt Nancy rewarded me with a refreshing soda pop along with an enjoyable loving visit.

An answered prayer also produced a full time job. In late 2008 I talked it over with Jennifer and made the decision to depart from my sales position with Ziglar, Inc. I continued to take pleasure in audio production projects with them. My colleagues there had become my family as they continue to be to this day.

My motivation for leaving sales was to increase my client base with the three-year-old production company that I had a real zeal for. I also wanted additional opportunities to speak with organizations on the significance of maintaining a winning vision.

I was reasonably successful in achieving both goals during the next year but I began desiring to return to full time employment with stable income. At that time our economy was unfortunately at its worst in several years, so I wasn't certain I should be back in sales, or I would have loved to have returned to my full time post with Ziglar. I began praying to Father God to please open up a door of an opportunity that would make use of my talents and skill sets.

During the same week I contacted three friends to see if they had time to get together for lunch. They agreed to a visit in a few days. So later in the week I hopped on the bus and rode over to Dallas Area Rapid Transit where my friends worked. I arrived a few minutes early and my friend, Doug Douglas, who is the director of Paratransit Services, called me into his office to introduce me to someone. Her name was Nancy Perkins and she was president of the Dallas Lighthouse for the Blind. I was delighted to hear Nancy's apparent passion coming right through her voice and also her vision for many improvements she planned on implementing at the Lighthouse.

After Nancy learned that I was a speaker and author she then invited me to address three separate groups at the Lighthouse. I immediately agreed to those engagements. During each visit I enjoyed getting to know all of the leaders with the Lighthouse quite well. I respected how much talent and enthusiasm there was in this place.

Following my third speaking opportunity I met again with Nancy Perkins. I asked her if the Lighthouse would benefit from a good communicator who could write and speak on our behalf, and even perform audio production for several useful assignments. We had a productive discussion regarding the many possibilities of this position that never existed here before. She thankfully hired me within a week.

I sure never thought that our planned lunch would have anything to do with future employment. I had no clue that Nancy Perkins would be where I was simply meeting up with friends. I had never applied at Dallas Lighthouse before and hadn't considered submitting an application there.

This full time employment has been completely fulfilling for me and has been beneficial for us all for more than two years already. I have gotten to utilize several of my God-given talents right here.

Incredibly, I have more opportunities now than I have ever had before, in speaking to groups on the subject of goal achievement. I also get to educate people about our many services and employment opportunities for the blind and visually impaired with our Dallas Lighthouse.

I continue to perform several production projects for clients during the evening, and on weekends. My audio business is gradually growing. Our God has proven to me again and again that he cares and truly answers our important prayers.

Chapter 22 Seeing Beyond the Blindness

Zig Ziglar caught my attention during my teenage years. Dad went to work with the Ziglar Corporation in 1981. Right before my junior year, Mom and Dad sent Brad and I to Zig Ziglar's Born to Win four-day seminar.

I have never encountered anyone so easy to pay attention to than Zig Ziglar, even when I was sixteen and tuning out much of what I should have been tuning in. Zig had a booming voice and used positive expressions to accentuate his points. For amusement, I used to do my best to imitate Zig to my brother Brad for a chuckle but knew that no one could do a Zig like Zig himself.

Blake and Zig at Born to Win in 1981.

Zig taught me to turn lemons into lemonade using the best of my ability as opposed to not trying to find a solution. He also taught me the importance of finding and uncovering the positive, even through the most negative of circumstances. My parents had taught me many of Zig's points but when you are a teenager it often takes another special someone to reinforce those "positives." Zig was my *someone* for certain. His teaching has paid off as people have often commented to me about my optimism and "Go get 'em" attitude.

Zig's sharing of his faith and his journeys of hardships and successes really helped me, along with tens of thousands of other people, to appreciate his relatable perception--it is not always a picnic in the park every day and how imperative it is that we remain faithful. He helped me in my practice of always wearing a smile, displaying optimism, and understanding the importance of being grateful. Here's another example in my life on how our God works in mysterious and positive ways.

In March 2006 I had the opportunity to be re-inspired by Zig Ziglar as I attended *Born to Win* for the second time in my life. It had been several years since Zig and I had an opportunity to talk about life due to me living in other cities and his working abroad a good part of the time. On the Monday following Zig's *Born to Win* seminar I was asked to lead the weekly devotions at the Ziglar Corporation. Right after our devotions and sharing some of my personal journey with the Ziglar staff I asked the Ziglar's if they would consider having me join their inspiring team. Just being in their presence was upbeat and encouraging. I already knew I wanted to be in sales and the opportunity of speaking has always seemed like a pleasurable privilege to me - which fortunately goes with the territory. I knew by working around Zig Ziglar and other great speakers on his team I would absolutely gain focus and become better through hearing and being around the pro's.

I am very pleased today to be a part of Zig's largest component of his corporation called *Ziglar: Inspiring True Performance*. I enjoy public speaking even more than before. I also have the pleasure of being the host of Zig Ziglar's free weekly Inspiring Podcast on his website: www.ziglar.com/podcast.

When our ten-minute, inspiring online broadcast began in September of 2006 we were excited to survey two thousand people punching in throughout the first week. We have increased substantially because of people's positive testimonies to their families, friends, and colleagues. We presently have over forty thousand people each week downloading Zig's Inspiring Podcast. I also enjoy using my broadcast talents with many brand new Ziglar projects.

Additionally, my job entails building relationships with companies that benefit greatly from the application of Zig Ziglar's Christian principles. We educate people using Zig's inspiring habits for setting goals and how to stay committed to achieving them. We also show people how important it is to shine at home as much as in your workplace and give life your best efforts at becoming a 24-hour champion.

Having a positive home life nearly always builds anyone up for success at having a productive and optimistic attitude at work.

The sales portion of my profession with the Ziglar team included telemarketing to public companies that weren't always expecting my call. People were typically pleasant and courteous when hearing from me just the same.

I did have an out-of-the-ordinary experience which was temporarily negative but it certainly had a completely positive outcome. It was, in fact, a true test of my desire to be a twenty-four hour champion. I want to share this life story with you because of the significant encouraging reinforcement I gained from this particular telephone call. I believe that this illustration will give you a chuckle, along with some reassurance, which is my favorite part of this narrative.

I spoke with a woman who was reasonably cordial, at least for the first few seconds of our conversation. She quickly inquired as to the nature of my call, which is common among the duties of people who answer a business telephone. I communicated that I desired to speak with someone in charge of team building in their organization. I further explained specific details regarding our Ziglar mission, which has been positively proven to be effective with increasing successes in several areas for big and small worldwide organizations. She advised she would try to locate someone I could speak with who best represented her company's leadership role. She asked me to please hold, and I then thanked her for her courtesy. The next thing I heard was the extremely noisy clattering of her telephone receiver. I mean she absolutely wanted me to hear every single whack. I couldn't help but want to hang on and hear what was going to happen next. She wasn't quite finished with me yet, as this discontented person proceeded to hang up her phone as deafeningly as possible.

This woman's earsplitting action was purely the opposite of kind; however, when I replay this comical call back in my mind, it is absolutely hilarious to me. When I share this story with people, I can't help but wonder if I am grinning in a silly way that looks like I were going to eat my breakfast banana sideways. I hoped, for this lady's sake, that her phone still worked properly. And I was very appreciative my telephone ear still worked. Following her rude retort, I couldn't help but laugh out loud at how I might have retaliated during my younger telemarketing years by taking way too much pleasure in my attempt at verbal destruction of this person.

When I was barely out of high school I secured a summer job as a telemarketer with a company called Thermaline. I sold energy saving replacement windows and fortunately performed well enough to be able to count on this redeeming occupation to financially compensate my occasional loll between jobs during my broadcast career.

I worked with several telemarketing establishments and all of these opportunities helped me gain knowledge on a range of trades. I sold anything from aluminum siding to insurance, along with other goods and services. I also raised thousands of dollars to help with preventing drug abuse.

The first reaction I might have encountered with this situation back in my less mature days would be to become irritated, then buzz her right back and chew her out with pointless verbiage. This could have made an unhelpfully permanent memory for both of us. Because I was proudly representing my friend and mentor, Zig Ziglar, and his Christian, caring corporation, I happily admit it helped me to respond calmly. So following her amusing telephone thrashing, I took a minute and tried to relate with her possible frustrations from receiving an uncalled-for telephone call. I also considered that she may have very well been having a difficult day for a completely different reason than my phone call. We've all been there before. Here comes my promised reinforcement portion of this story.

The very next telephone call I made was to an upbeat person, who was very nice, appreciative, and completely helpful. Following my conversation with this kind contact, I set the phone down as I immediately realized I had earned two reassuring rewards. Because I chose to not react in anger, I could now celebrate that our Lord swiftly positioned an encouraging person right into my life to directly redeem those disapproving actions from the character on the call right before. Second was a feeling of relief which came from having no regrets from negative reactions. Wow, was I ever pleased at how this event had turned out. I quickly said a prayer of genuine thanks for the lesson, which had really increased my armor.

Today, I pray I will always be able to recognize the fortification I receive, as well as to take a minute to express my gratitude to God each time he comes through and energizes me at just the right time. I really needed an upbeat call following such a downbeat one, which was exactly what I got. I continue to learn daily that this positive response from God happens often when we try to keep our cool and maintain hope for our next action or event.

I've of course observed that being a consistent champion is not an effortless mission. I believe this is why God reminded me with this case in point of how doing our best to become 24-hour champions is an exciting and very rewarding challenge that we can all work toward achieving. I try to become closer each day in being a more dependable champion. It certainly pays us to be reliable and to give God our very best efforts. Being a team player with the Ziglar Corporation allowed me to continue to grow and develop as a Christian man and as a motivator for people.

Two years ago I was hired to be on the Executive Team as Director of Communications for the Dallas Lighthouse for the Blind. It is a thrill to observe the dozens of life transformations of people who are blind or visually impaired. One of my favorite assignments is interviewing our associates on audio and then transforming those interviews into written stories which shine a positive spotlight on their contributions. I call these stories our High Profile Contributor of the Week. I wanted their true stories to be a morale booster, and it has been precisely that. We've all gotten to know each other even better because of their summaries.

Our Dallas Lighthouse specializes in jobs and job training for people who are blind and low vision between the ages of 18, and 70 years old. We also have an outreach program called Serving Our Seniors, for people who lose their sight between the age of 55 and 95 years old. We are able to not only encourage them, but also show them how to use the best

Dallas Lighthouse
for the Blind
focus on opportunity

assistive technology for their specific needs. We serve over 700 seniors each year. It is a big blessing to observe the drastic progress taking place in their lives. Many of these people thought their life would stop because their sight did. They are thrilled to be proven incorrect on their assumptions.

Another pleasurable component of my assignment is being a spokesperson who shares our vision with all types and ages of people. I enjoy improving mindsets on what blindness truly means.

It is my goal to travel around the country and provide inspiration and encouragement to others through speaking engagements and book signings.

I have been fortunate enough to experience reaching my sales goals and writing this book, and I hope that my true-life stories inspire everyone with and without physical challenges.

Chapter 23 Living as a Christian

Three weeks before my ninth birthday I drove with my parents to attend church at the large Lakeview Christian Temple in Indianapolis. I'll never forget this wonderful Wednesday on the first day of August. What a superb way to begin my month.

I heard that it was going to be a very special event as Charles and Francis Hunter, known as The Happy Hunters, were going to be at this grand church to share their remarkable testimony. I loved it when I could listen to Christians enlighten us with their real-life stories.

Francis had been a two-pack-a-day cigarette smoker who previously was popular for having such a gravitating but tainted sense of humor. She had a big booming voice to help her belt out the best jokes while frequenting the bars. However, when she gave her life to Jesus everything changed for the very best. Francis kept her wonderful sense of humor; it was just without the filth. She and Charles became born again Christians with a passion to share their story of transformation.

Many people I have talked to about being a Christian are fearful of taking on a dull personality because they are deceived into believing they are required to lower their level of enjoyment in life. The Happy Hunters were on an exciting mission to prove that Christians can literally be the happiest people on earth, and they sure sold me.

Even as a young boy, I was as intrigued as I could be by their humorous and inspiring stories that I enjoyed that day. I desired a spiritual change in my youthful life. The Hunters had never been healthier or happier and did not lose one ounce of their people-attracting personalities.

A few years later I understood God's will more clearly. I was baptized in water for the remission of my sins. "What would Jesus do?" is my favorite bumper sticker. Though I regrettably do not always conduct myself in the correct manner, I truly try each day to improve and to live life in the following of Jesus Christ. I am learning to wisely use the power of choice and free will that God has given me.

It is a simple truth that if we let the Holy Spirit be our agent of salvation, everything for us will begin to change for the better.

Some people make choices to be takers and breakers. I am committed to being a giver and a builder. I understand that I will not be perfect here on Earth, but I want to be as much like Jesus as often as possible.

I can certainly make the following testimony after having known Jesus for more than 30 years: When I am trying with all of my might to live right, by praying often and working to make a positive difference with my example and workmanship, I have many more green light days with more and more life situations going the right way.

I am happier and more productive when I put God first in my life. Yes, I recognize that there are good people, who have not made this critical decision, which I am certain will affect the rest of their lives forever. Therefore, I want to prove with my best example that it is the greatest and most important decision to make for all of us. This is also my responsibility as a Christian because nothing in the world is more enormous, and therefore important, than our eternity.

Sometimes when I am having this discussion with someone, they will ask me, "What if all of this is a big fairy tale, and there is no such place as Heaven or Hell and we simply die when our life is done?" So, let's go ahead and imagine for a minute that Heaven and Hell are only a myth. Then, what are the advantages of being a Christian? For one, I have enjoyed integrating richer relationships into my life because of my distinctive decision to live as a Christian. My Christian friends have consistently proven time and time again that they are a great deal more dependable, and also abundantly encouraging. Christians truly care more because Jesus Christ cared more, and we fortunately have complete access to Jesus' glorious help with becoming more Christ-like as our commitment ignites our improved attitude.

I have complete hope that every non-believer will at least consider these few important life-changing reasons that I celebrate daily. Even if this is only a fifty percent possibility, why take a gamble on our eternity? I have absolutely concluded that it is not worth me doubting the Bible, even if I am only taking a fifty percent chance of plugging my soul into a painful torment forever. I know that after everything I have heard and read regarding Hell, that if there is even a half of a likelihood this tormenting place exists, our forever life is certainly not something worth taking that gamble on.

When I imagine that people's lost souls may be burning eternally and they will be antagonized by Hell's demons, I want to do all that I am able to during my earthly life to prevent people from having this horrible occasion without end.

Now, let's look at the exciting side. I read and hear that Heaven will be greater than we can possibly see in our mind's eye. I believe I will enjoy having my eyesight perfectly restored during this inconceivable, forever celebration that we Christians will have with our Lord.

Even if there is not a Heaven or Hell, what do we really lose by doing our best to be Christ-like? I'm certain that no one could give enough reasons to forfeit our pleasurable eternity in Heaven with our best friend and savior Jesus, and our big Christian family. I hope we ask ourselves, on the most serious note, is it worth taking this risk by being a nonbeliever? Thank goodness many of us choose to say absolutely not. I personally believe I'm getting a much better quality deal right here on earth because of the choice I made over thirty years ago.

I hope these thoughts for starters make superb sense to open minded people. When Christians read God's word and pray several times each day, our creator's way quickly becomes our way of living. He truly knows all. I am reminded of a verse from John 15:5. "I am the vine; you are the branches. If a man remains in me and I in him, he will bear much fruit; apart from me you can do nothing."

I am a happier person when I follow God's will. I try to stay away from situations that can become stumbling blocks for me. I enjoy a further fulfilled life, along with a true peace, when I try my best to do what God desires me to accomplish. I realize that as long as I am here on earth it is quite easy to trip up, especially if I am choosing to remain in those tempting and disapproving surroundings.

Life is good and life is valuable. I believe I enjoy life so much because of the relationship I have with Jesus Christ. When I understood John 15:5, I became even more excited by Philippians 4:13, which reads, "I can do everything through him who gives me strength."

Following Mom's tremendous news regarding Doratha's dose of inspiration from the most recent bicycle expedition, Dad found an appropriate Bible verse which he read to me that completely relates to our account of unquestioning teamwork. This relevant verse is from Proverbs 3:5-6. "Trust in the Lord with all your heart, mind and strength; and lean not unto your own understanding. In all thy ways acknowledge him and he shall direct thy paths."

Just as I trusted my earthly father that wonderful day while peddling my bike to his lead, I am learning more and more each day to trust in our heavenly father for more competent caring leadership than we can possibly picture in our minds.

I may never have the opportunity to see anything or anyone in my lifetime until I reach Heaven. I hope you will be there because I certainly desire to meet you, as well as see you.

Final Thoughts

As I write this last chapter in reflection, I am grateful for four things in my upbringing that grew me to become who I am today.

First, my rich family and church traditions helped me develop Christian roots that eventually began to blossom and flower in my life. I am thankful for those memories of Christian fellowship, bible study, and prayer. Thankfully, I did not stray too far from those wonderful traditions that I continue to cherish today.

Second, it is easy for me now to appreciate rich Christian experiences such as Sunday school, daily vacation bible school, church services, youth outings, church camp, and dozens of other things that allowed me to be in fellowship with other Christian friends.

Third, faith comes by hearing and hearing the Holy Scriptures. Through the years scriptures I heard and heard again from pastors, Sunday school teachers, family members, tapes, Christian radio, or television and in many other ways began to penetrate my spirit and mind. They say the word of God does not return void so I am grateful for knowing the Word of Truth. I eagerly acknowledge that I am hungrier to hear the Word of Truth today than ever before and I need that certainty to be a success in Christ.

Finally, I have come a long way in knowing what I believe and what I don't believe. In this knowledge, I have come to learn to reason together with God and the Holy Scriptures. I do not fully trust in leaning on my own understanding. So, I am trying to know and more fully understand God's word so I can wisely use my reasoning abilities and power of choice.

I wrote this book to try and challenge us all to be grateful for the lives we have and for the hardships we endure to make us stronger in our hearts. I also want to encourage you parents who have children with disabilities to please coach your kids from babies to adults to focus on their abilities, and not center their attention on their disability. This positive perception can make all of the helpful difference in their world. In addition, please do your very best with treating the extra challenges as blessings and not as hindrances.

My Mom and Dad exerted extra effort, created expectations for me, and even provided me opportunities to experience a life not much different from my siblings. They were my encouragers, not my discouragers. It is my hope you, as parents, are the encouragers for your children. After all, if you are not then who will be?

Mom and Dad's example of deep love and abiding faith in Jesus Christ not only sustained them throughout the two extremely difficult months when I lost my sight, but it enabled them to become stronger Christians and better parents as well.

During my surgeries, Mom and Dad spent considerable time in the prayer room at the hospital. I have since learned that they had dedicated my life to the Lord and asked God to use this tragedy in my life to bring honor and glory to God.

As an adult Christian, I have been increasingly telling my story in order to encourage parents, children, and those facing struggles in life that there is great and enduring hope in the Lord Jesus Christ.

As I reflect on this life story of family faith, I easily understand that it is God's purpose that I have been totally sightless since the age of 10 months, so that in later years I can proclaim the good news of Jesus and witness to the power of Christian parenting.

There are people who ask me, "Didn't you have any negative experiences in your life?" I have had a number of those experiences, as we all do. But as I have reflected back through my life, the upbeat situations have outweighed the downbeat ones by a big margin. I would estimate it to be about three good to one not so good.

As many of you reading this are joining me in reflecting upon your lives, I can personally say that there are things that really added value to my existence. I confess that I made some decisions, said words, and displayed some actions for which I have been compelled to ask the Lord for forgiveness. As Zig Ziglar says, "It is not where you start in life but how you finish that makes the difference."

I want to finish strong. How about you? May God bless each and every one of you!

Further Information

If you would like to comment on my book or inquire about booking a personal appearance, you may do so at the following:

<u>blake@blakelindsay.com</u>
214-207-6972

I look forward to hearing from you.

www.ingramcontent.com/pod-product-compliance
Lightning Source LLC
Chambersburg PA
CBHW021015090426
42738CB00007B/794